Union with God

Father Gabriel of St. Mary Magdalen, OCD

Union with God

According to St. John of the Cross

Translated from the Italian
by Sister Miriam of Jesus, OCD

Carmel of Maria Regina Eugene, Oregon,
with the kind permission of
The Carmel of St. Joseph Rome, Italy

**SPIRITUAL DIRECTION
SERIES**

SOPHIA INSTITUTE PRESS

Manchester, New Hampshire

Scripture quotations in this work are taken from the *Revised Standard Version of the Bible: Catholic Edition*, copyright © 1965, 1966 the Division of Christian Education of the National Council of the Churches of Christ in the United States of America. Used by permission. All rights reserved.

Sophia Institute Press
Box 5284, Manchester, NH 03108
1-800-888-9344

www.SophiaInstitute.com

Sophia Institute Press® is a registered trademark of Sophia Institute.

Library of Congress Cataloging-in-Publication Data
Names: Gabriele di Santa Maria Maddalena, Father, author.
Title: Union with God : according to St. John of the Cross / Father Gabriel of St. Mary Magdalen, OCD ; translated from the Italian by Sister Miriam of Jesus, OCD, Carmel of Maria Regina Eugene, Oregon, with the kind permission of The Carmel of St. Joseph Rome, Italy.
Other titles: Unione con Dio secondo san Giovanni della Croce. English
Description: Manchester : Sophia Institute Press, 2019. | Originally published: Eugene, Or. : Carmel of Maria Regina, 1990. | Includes bibliographical references. | Summary: "The author explains St. John of the Cross's teaching on how every person can attain union with God"— Provided by publisher.
Identifiers: LCCN 2019022901 | ISBN 9781622828586 (paperback)
Subjects: LCSH: Mystical union—History of doctrines—16th century. | John of the Cross, Saint, 1542-1591. | John of the Cross, Saint, 1542-1591.
Classification: LCC BT767.7 .G3313 2019 | DDC 248.2/2—dc23
LC record available at https://lccn.loc.gov/2019022901

3rd printing

Contents

Introduction

On December 14, 1591, just after midnight, St. John of the Cross died in Úbeda, Spain, at the early age of forty-nine. In his own words, he went to "sing matins in heaven," where the darkness of faith gave way to the light of glory and union with God became eternal beatitude.

Union with God had been the hidden treasure and the pearl of great price for which he sacrificed everything else and to which he showed others the way by his teaching, his spiritual direction, and his writings. His gentle single-mindedness is expressed in one of the maxims we find among his writings: "One human thought alone is worth more than the whole world; hence, God alone is worthy of it." This profound respect for every person is reflected in his ministry. While, by reason of the various offices he held in the Discalced Carmelite Order, his teaching and direction were addressed primarily to his brothers and sisters in Carmel, we know that he gave much of his time to the instruction and spiritual direction of the poor and the simple people in the neighborhood of Duruelo in Segovia.

St. John was canonized in 1726 and proclaimed a doctor of the Church in 1926, but he has never become what one might call a "popular" saint. His austere image and the language—such as "the *all* and the *nothing*" and the "*dark night*"—associated with his writings tend to put people off.

The year 1926, during which St. John was proclaimed a doctor of the Church, also marked the beginning of Father Gabriel's ministry as teacher and spiritual director in Rome. Like St. John, his teaching and spiritual direction were primarily addressed to Carmelite students and to some communities of Carmelite nuns. I had the privilege of attending his lectures in spiritual theology for two years. What impressed one most was the enthusiastic conviction with which he spoke. And that was particularly true when he illustrated the universal call to holiness and showed how the teaching of St. John of the Cross was so relevant and valid for all. Later, when he was much in demand as a lecturer and a spiritual director, it was this same message that he brought to the hundreds of laypeople who attended his conferences throughout Italy and in other European centers. And the more he studied St. John of the Cross, the more he became convinced that here was a saint and doctor of the Church who deserved to be more widely known, whose writings contained such clear and relevant teaching for people of every walk of life.

In this book, Father Gabriel set out to do exactly that. *Union with God* was written for all those, especially laypersons, who are sincerely seeking God. Father Gabriel was well aware that many people who pick up the writings of St. John for the first time are put off by the austere, uncompromising logic of *The Ascent of Mount Carmel* and *The Dark Night of the Soul*, the first of the saint's writings they will come up against in the various editions of his works. Father Gabriel's advice is to begin with *The Spiritual Canticle*, where they will find a description of the fullness of life that God offers to those who seek Him. Only when they have gotten a glimpse of the goal will they be prepared to undertake the journey of faith and renunciation that leads to perfect love.

Introduction

Union with God is a compendium of St. John's teaching, presented by one who lived it before he wrote it. It is a handbook, a guide on the journey of faith and on the way of prayer and Christian perfection to total conformity with God's will. Laypeople will find it both helpful and encouraging, not because it waters down in any way St. John's teaching, but because of the clarity with which it applies to their state of life the demands of detachment and renunciation, without which total surrender to the action of the Holy Spirit is not possible.

Like any handbook or guide, this is not a book to be read quickly and then put aside. It is for readers who are committed to a genuine life of prayer and Christian perfection and who will continue to consult it as they continue on their ascent to holiness.

For many people, this English translation may be their first acquaintance with the teaching of St. John of the Cross. It is to be hoped that this book will dispel any fears that keep them from reading his works and discovering for themselves the beauty and depth of spirituality they contain. If it succeeds in that, I think that both the author of the Italian original and Sister Miriam, who did the translation, will feel fully rewarded.

—Father Finian Monahan, OCD

Preface

This book owes its origin to the request of the publisher Salani, who wanted a volume for his new series of books that would present to persons living in the world the spiritual life in that integral fullness with which St. John of the Cross, doctor of the Church and master of union with God, offers it.

Having to speak of the doctrine of St. John of the Cross to persons who live in the world, I did not want to present it in an attenuated form; to me, that would have seemed like a betrayal.

There are not two doctrines of St. John of the Cross, one for religious and one for seculars. There is only one, which applies to all Christians indiscriminately and requires not a special state of life but only a disposition of will—namely, the disposition of not wanting to be confined to mediocrity and therefore of not refusing generous renunciation at every privation required for attaining a more intimate union with God. In other words, the doctrine of the saint applies to all souls who do not want to live a Christian life by halves, but who want to correspond in full measure to their vocation as children of God and truly give God the place in their hearts that belongs to Him: the place of absolute preference above all others.

God does not forbid us to love creatures; on the contrary, He often commands us to do so, but He wants us to love them in conformity to His will and without attaching our hearts to them, in such a way that, while enjoying the use of created goods, we do not refuse God the preference owed to Him.

The world suffers and feels itself out of balance because it is alienated from God. Unfortunately, good souls are also far from Him, in the sense that they are not sufficiently united to Him; and that results from the fact that they live too immersed in creatures. Good souls grieve because today the world is far from God, and they believe that they themselves do not belong to the world either; but the world is the totality of individuals, and therefore, the practical way to lead the world to God is first to return to Him ourselves.

If we want our personal return to God to be effective and fruitful, however, not only for ourselves, but also for others, it must not end halfway but must go on to the goal—that is, to union with God. To this, St. John of the Cross shows just one way, precisely because it is the only way, and there is not another that can be shown to souls who live in the world. All the same, in expounding the nature of this way, one can and ought to take into account the particular conditions of persons who live in the world. That is our very purpose in the work we are presenting.

St. John of the Cross foresaw that this doctrine of his would not be to everyone's taste, because all do not feel called to rise from mediocrity.

A noble soul, however, finds that a mediocre life is hardly worth the pain of being lived. And so, to such souls, as he says in the prologue to *The Ascent of Mount Carmel*, he presents his doctrine, "a doctrine substantial and solid, as much for the one as for the others, namely, for seculars and for religious, provided that they want to pass through the spiritual spoliation which is herein described."[1]

---

[1] St. John of the Cross, prologue to *The Ascent of Mount Carmel*, no. 8.
N.B. The quotations are the personal translations of Father Gabriel.

Hence, we wanted to present it as it is, without any diminution, because this is necessary in our century, which is drying up in mediocrity. To this doctrine, however hidden it may be, "total" souls are aspiring. May God raise up a great number of these to the benefit of all.

—Father Gabriel of St. Mary Magdalen, OCD
November 1945

Union with God

1

Master of the Contemplative Life

We believe that to present St. John of the Cross as a master of the contemplative life — that is, of the life that seeks intimate union with God — is to respond to a need of the present Christian generation.

The truly Christian soul, through the painful fortunes of war,[2] has come to understand better that His kingdom is not of this world and has felt his aspirations reborn toward a more stable reality. Profound souls, having experienced the fleeting nature of pleasures and of human security, have experienced the need of something more solid on which to lean, and they have realized that they ought to give the Lord a greater place in their lives than that which they have left Him up to this time. They understand that they have remained at a distance from Him for too long, and now they are seeking to draw near to Him. Thus, they very often hunger and thirst for God and wish to be united with Him, persuaded that in Him they will find what they had in vain expected from creatures.

But often, such noble souls ask themselves anxiously if these spontaneous aspirations of close friendship with the Lord and of union with God are realizable. Might not this also be a vain

---

[2] Father Gabriel wrote after the Second World War. — Ed.

expectation destined to be frustrated, an enterprise that is bound to fail? Might not their ideal have been placed too high? And in what way can this ideal possibly be attained?

All these souls need a light to illumine them, a guide who will take them by the hand and lead them. At this point, we would like to indicate such a light and such a guide by speaking of St. John of the Cross, master of the contemplative life and of intimate union with God.

To show that souls have real need of his teaching, I will reply briefly to three questions:

• Who is St. John of the Cross?
• Of which souls was he the master?
• What is meant by the contemplative life?

The Master

Who is St. John of the Cross?

To reply to this question of historical order, I will not sketch even a brief biography of the saint; instead, I will endeavor to delineate one of his characteristics that will make his mission to souls quickly understood.

I will say, however, that he was a theologian of Teresian spirituality. In other words, he was the student, the scholar, the one who reduced to an organic body of doctrine founded on solid principles of theology, the teachings on living a perfect and holy life with which Teresa of Jesus guided her spiritual daughters to the heights of intimacy with God in the first monasteries of the Carmelite Reform.[3]

[3] St. John of the Cross worked with St. Teresa of Avila to reform the Carmelite Order. St. Teresa's efforts sought to restore the austerity and contemplative character of Carmelite life. Reformed Carmelites

In fact, in 1562, the great saint of Avila, desirous of creating an atmosphere where the best aids to enable souls to attain an intimate union with God would be found, enclosed herself with a few ardent souls in a monastery of strict enclosure, organizing the life of her nuns with a collection of laws that are a marvel of wisdom and discretion. By order of her spiritual directors who had known how much she was enlightened by God, she wrote, for the formation of the persons confided to her, a few books of spiritual education that were destined for centuries afterward to be the admiration of all those who were studying the concrete dealings of the soul with God. But naturally, these writings, being the fruit of a genial intellect enriched with heavenly gifts, were not presented in scientific form. They are filled with profound intuitions, but they do not have a systematic development, and for that reason, they need further clarification.

The humble Teresa was too intelligent not to take this into account, and therefore, especially when her Reform began to expand, she wanted very much to have the Fathers also in her family — that is, religious priests who would live the same life as her daughters, a life of recollection, directed to the search for intimacy with God. She wanted these to possess a culture capable of throwing theological light on the way of life the saint had so well organized in practice.

The Lord responded magnificently to this desire of hers, giving her as her first son in her religious family, a priest, an eminent theologian whose profound doctrine would one day merit for him the title of doctor of the Church. He was John of the Cross.

The Lord wanted him to be instructed and formed in the life of the Teresian Reform by the foundress herself, who took him with her for the foundation of a new monastery at Valladolid. After that,

were known as Discalced, or barefoot, Carmelites, because they wore sandals instead of shoes and stockings. —Ed.

he became the spiritual father, first of the saint herself and then of her Carmelite nuns. Even while he was the spiritual director for the first time of a Teresian monastery, he began to compose *The Ascent of Mount Carmel* and to write a commentary on *The Spiritual Canticle*, which he had already composed, two works that are among the most elevated that the Church possesses in her treasury of mystical writings.

In these, St. John of the Cross reveals what a profound theologian of the life of union with God he is; that is, he discloses the life that leads to this union. He not only bases his exposition on practical experience, as does Teresa of Jesus, but he establishes the whole synthesis of his teachings on the solid base of the principles of theology, thus constructing a body of doctrine that is well proportioned, through the balance of its various parts, and luminous, through the clarity of his reasoning. The saint is not content with "affirming," as is Teresa, guided by her marvelous intuitions; he expounds, he reasons, he gives arguments, and thus he convinces and makes one understand the necessity of what he teaches. John of the Cross possesses and communicates the essence of the spiritual ways—in particular, of those that lead the soul to a profound intimacy with God.

It is clear that such a saint is capable of guiding souls who, in our day, are thirsting for union with God. Yet the thought might come to our minds that his teachings were directed solely to religious and therefore do not pertain to people living in the world. For that reason, we wish to answer another question as well: "Of which souls was John of the Cross the master?"

The Disciples of the Saint

Someone might think that St. John of the Cross was a director reserved exclusively to friars and nuns, but that does not entirely correspond to historical truth: he always dealt with secular persons, and the relations he had with them went so far as to be a real and actual education in the highest spiritual life.

Together with Father Anthony, he initiated the work of the Reform among the Fathers in a small country house that, like the stable of Bethlehem, became the Lord's dwelling place, since it was transformed, in part, into a tiny church, very soon frequented by the peasants of the countryside.

John then gave himself to an intense apostolic life among those good, simple people, who were, it seems, little instructed in matters of religion. And no sooner were they in contact with his ardent soul than these upright hearts were inflamed, and the little chapel of the Carmelite Fathers became witness to the prolonged prayers and the works of penance performed by those whom the saint had converted to the Lord.

It was not only the country people who came under the influence of his great soul. The students and professors of the university cities of Alcalá and Baeza, where the new Reform, to satisfy the need of its members for theological knowledge, had opened houses, were impressed by the extraordinary gifts of mind and heart that he revealed in his conversation. Consequently, it was not John who went in search of people; it was they who came to find him at the convent. He was a priest: How could he refuse himself to souls who needed him?

Obviously, his first obligations were to his religious family. In the monasteries in which he was superior, he had devoted sons rather than disciples. In the convents where he was spiritual director, he had many daughters who lived as he did, a life consecrated solely to the search for union with God. He was conscious of his grave duty as educator, especially in those first years of the Reform, in which he needed to give solidarity to the foundation for the future and to create the new spirit that was to animate the family. In the houses of the Reform, John felt himself completely a "father"; he intuitively sensed that the spirit was expected to come from him. His inventive and genial temperament enabled him to find every means to cultivate the spirit of the religious confided to him: poetry, maxims, drawings, explanations, preaching; everything served as a stimulus to live a deeper, more generous interior life. All this also served as a light to penetrate deeper into the life of the spirit, which can reach sublime heights, where God communicates Himself and becomes the life of the soul. Sons and daughters were avid to hear him, taking notes during his sermons, interrogating him in private conversations and then begging him: "Father, write this down for us!"

Thus were born those works of his that have become immortal: *The Ascent of Mount Carmel*, in which he expounds, to the soul that desires to "ascend," those practices and attitudes with which it will better make its way to union; and *The Dark Night of the Soul*, in which he describes how the Lord comes into contact with the soul that is seeking Him. John enables the soul to understand that the darkness of the ways of God ought not to frighten or discourage it but are indispensable conditions for greater progress. Then also, in *The Spiritual Canticle*, its delicate verses composed amid the distressing circumstances of his imprisonment in Toledo, he sang of the expansion of the soul that has arrived at divine union. At the request of Mother Anne of Jesus, he commented on these verses, first orally at Beas, then in writing at Granada.

Did he, then, always write just for nuns and friars? No, not only for them; in fact, the most elevated of his works, *The Living Flame of Love*, was composed of strophes and comments for a lady of the nobility, a benefactress of the order, Doña Ana de Peñalosa. This lady and her daughter often visited the saint, and he taught them a doctrine that was no different from that which he preached at the monasteries, and therefore with the same instructions about total abnegation that leads to perfect union with God. And in fact, Doña Ana was seen one day by the nuns of Granada kneeling at the feet of the saint while he, with his eyes fixed on heaven, hammered the hard but liberating sentence: "Nothing, nothing, nothing, even to leaving your skin and everything for Christ!"

So, it was not only the crumbs from his sumptuous table that the saint allotted to seculars: it was his doctrine in its entirety that he was able to adapt to their situations, knowing as he did that they are not the same as those of religious. They live in other surroundings, they have other duties and tasks, but they likewise have immortal souls, clothed with the same divine grace, souls that eagerly desire union with the same God. John never forgot this. Religious are not the only ones called to sanctity; this is the sublime vocation of all Christians. Pope Pius XI repeated it incessantly during his pontificate, meriting the gratitude of all Catholics. Why, then, should seculars be less eager for sanctity than religious?

True, it is not as easy to become holy in the world as in the cloister; but even in the cloister, one does not become holy without much labor and suffering, without overcoming many difficulties and repugnances. In the world, these will be different from those met with in the cloister; but as in the cloister, so also in the world, they exist only to be surmounted. They will be surmounted by using the same fundamental means: prayer and sacrifice.

Are seculars perhaps not able to pray? A mother of a family who raises many children for the glory of the Lord will not, it is true, have time to spend long hours in church, but will she not be able, perhaps even while caring for her children, to raise her heart to God, to live in His presence, to offer Him her weariness, her anxieties, and her troubles? With a little goodwill, may she not find a half hour in which, while not interrupting all her occupations, she can apply herself more directly to conversation with God?

Is it not the same for workmen?

I passed some years of my early priesthood among young workers. I still remember with emotion the prayer with which they daily made the offering of their day of fatigue, thus transforming it into scrolls of incense that rose unceasingly to the divine throne. And they were not only words. The Jocists — that is to say, the Belgian Association of Young Catholic Workers, since become international — likewise has its saints. The true Jocist makes his meditation and his daily sacrifices, practices, and mortifications, although not in the same way as the religious does. There really are "total" souls in all classes of society.

Truly "total" were those souls who spontaneously formed a group around the saint, avid for his doctrine, which recognized no half measures. Why in the world, then, should there be mediocre Christians? The secular is not encircled like the monk by surroundings that are suited to sanctifying people; quite otherwise! Too often, it is a depressing environment, full of temptations, but for that very reason, it will be more meritorious for him to create a spiritual atmosphere constituted from the good habits with which he steels himself against the influences of vice and nourishes holier aspirations to union with God. In this, St. John of the Cross aided all the souls he directed, whether laypeople or religious.

Union and intimacy with God are not reserved to religious. God is the Father of all and desires that all Christians live with Him as true sons and daughters. And how can they be such if they do not tend to intimacy with him?

St. John of the Cross indicates to everyone the direct way that leads there, and we present him therefore as master of contemplative life.

But what does the contemplative life signify?

The Contemplative Life

The contemplative life is not to be confused with contemplation. This latter is indeed a gift of God, which He alone can measure to our capacity, and He gives it "to whom He wills, when He wills, and as He wills," as St. Teresa of Jesus loved to repeat. But it is not the same way with the contemplative life.

By "the contemplative life" is meant that form of Christian life that directly seeks intimacy with God. The old distinction of the Christian life into active and contemplative is based on the twofold means by which we can cultivate in ourselves the virtue of charity, having these two objects: God and neighbor.

Everyone knows that Christian perfection—that is to say, sanctity—consists essentially in the perfection of the virtue of charity, but precisely, this virtue, having two objects, can be cultivated in us by service of the neighbor for love of God, or by the direct search for the fullness of the love of God. The effort to serve one's neighbor constitutes the active life; the direct search for the love of God constitutes the contemplative life. And just as love tends to stabilize intimate relations with the person loved, this seeking of the fullness of the love of God can very well be characterized as the search for divine intimacy. It is commonly said that he who seeks intimacy with God gives himself to the contemplative life.

For this search to be efficacious, however, the most suitable method should be used to procure it. The means best adapted to deepening this intimacy with God in the soul are principally two; and the whole of tradition indicates them as prayer and mortification.

Mortification, also called abnegation, renunciation, and sacrifice, having for effect the detachment of the soul from created things, frees the soul's capacity to love from every obstacle that could retard its impulse toward God. Prayer, which consists essentially in an affectionate colloquy with God, kindles divine love in the heart, where mortification has prepared the place. If we detach our heart from created things, it is not simply to place it in a void, but to fill it with love. Taking into account the necessary use of these two instruments to attain intimacy with God, we will be able to describe the contemplative life more specifically, saying that it is "the form of Christian life that tends to intimacy with God by means of the assiduous exercise of prayer and mortification."

You will perhaps be surprised to learn that the contemplative life consists in this alone, and you may ask: "What has such a life to do with contemplation, since, after all, the word 'contemplative' obviously alludes to that? Does contemplation, then, having nothing whatever to do with it?"

We repeat that contemplation is not to be confused with the contemplative life; nevertheless, the latter has a close relationship with the former: the contemplative life prepares, disposes, and orients the soul toward contemplation; more than that, when it comes to be lived with fervor, it is habitually followed by contemplation. In other words, the contemplative life leads to contemplation, which is the aim and end of the contemplative life.

So then, what is contemplation?

I will say that it is a particular way of knowing God whereby that intimacy with God to which the contemplative life aspires is best achieved.

I am speaking of a "particular way of knowing" God, because God can be known in different ways. There are two rather different ones: the first is the *intellectual* way, which is verified by means of the operation of our intellect; the second is the *experiential* way, which is ascertained fundamentally by means of a love that proceeds from our will.

Let me explain further.

We know God first of all with intellectual, or rather conceptual, knowledge — that is, by means of the ideas that we form of Him. Let us note that this way of knowing God is the principal, and to this we ought always to return; intellectual knowledge of God nourishes and restrains our contemplative knowledge, which instead, as we shall see, is not conceptual and does not proceed by means of ideas.

From childhood, we have learned that God is our Creator and Lord, who created us out of nothing and on whom we are totally dependent. This God of ours is Triune—that is, in the unity of the divine nature there are three Persons; one of these became incarnate for our redemption; we are called to live one day in the company of this Most Holy Trinity, in eternal beatitude. We have known all these truths intellectually—that is, by means of the ideas that have been given to us and that we ourselves have formed of the divine reality. Seeking to know, we form concepts that we progressively elaborate; and the clearer and more precise these concepts become, the better we know the divine reality through them. These better-known truths move us, then, to a greater love for God, since we understand better the immense love that leads Him to want to receive us eternally into His company and to want to redeem us from sin—which prevents our union with Him—which He accomplished with the most painful death of His divine Incarnate Son.

Meditative mental prayer consists basically in this intellectual knowledge of God; in it we seek to understand better the mysteries of our holy religion, and from these mysteries better understood, we derive new incentives for love. That is why meditation is so fruitful in the spiritual life.

Nevertheless, intellectual knowledge, although precious, is not the only means by which we can know God. We can also know Him by means of love, with knowledge of an experiential nature; in this, however, the concepts no longer serve in a direct manner, and precisely for that reason such knowledge always has something indistinct and obscure about it for us. Deep and intense love of God does not directly give us new ideas of God, but it communicates to us that which can be called the "sense of God." With this sense, the soul realizes, not with reasonings or proofs, but in a way, so to speak, experientially, that He is so different from all creatures, so unique, so great as indeed to merit all the affection of our hearts.

This is verified especially when the soul enjoys the love that St. John of the Cross calls passive — that is, the love in which the soul is not only moved toward God of its own initiative but also feels itself drawn by God. As St. Teresa of Jesus explains, describing the prayer of quiet, which is one of the first stages of contemplation, the soul feels that its will becomes a prisoner of God and it would not be possible to love anything else. It feels so content with its God that a great peace invades it. It feels in its right place, in a contact of love with Him, who has created it for Himself. It could say with St. Augustine: "Thou hast made us for Thyself, O Lord, and our hearts are restless until they rest in Thee" (*Confessions* I, 1). Here, indeed, it rests in God and feels that it could be completely satisfied. Thus, by means of love, the soul arrives at a certain experience of God, which is then reflected in the intellect, without, however, taking there the form of concepts.

The soul experiences great difficulty in manifesting what it feels, and this difficulty comes from the fact that it is a matter of knowledge acquired not by means of ideas or intellectual concepts but through love, and from this is derived only a profound yet indefinite sense of the divine grandeur. Our words are formed to the extent of our concepts and are adapted, therefore, with difficulty to express what ordinarily does not pertain to ideas. Therefore, the soul has much difficulty in speaking when it wants to render an account of what takes place within it and needs to have recourse to figures and comparisons, as if to suggest what it cannot succeed in expressing.

It is not to be supposed that the difficulty in communicating to others the knowledge that is effected through love confers on this knowledge a kind of inferiority. For this kind also is the supreme knowledge to which man can attain and to which, we hope, we ourselves will one day also attain: the beatific vision of heaven. In heaven, we shall see God as He is, with an immediate intellectual experience, which is called clear vision of God in Himself. That is to say, we shall see—not that we shall be able to contain Him in concept: no human concept is capable of expressing the infinite divine perfection that we shall contemplate face-to-face. It follows that that which is most fundamental in eternal life, and which constitutes the most intimate joy of the blessed—the divine Object in its proper essence—is something that cannot be expressed, precisely because we can only speak of and communicate that of which we can form a concept; and of this (divine Object) it is not possible to form an adequate concept.

No one of the blessed can express to another what he most intimately experiences, for there, what is most profound in our beatitude will take place between God and each of us, between the human person and the divine Persons. That is the supreme grandeur of the human person: to be called to live eternally in intimate companionship with his God; alone with God alone, in an inexpressible contact with Him. Thus, one understands that the society of the blessed in heaven, however pleasant, constitutes only an accidental happiness, added to that essential one that we will experience by being with God and in enjoying Him.

Truly God has made us for Himself, and how well they act who on earth already seek to live intimately with Him! This is exactly what contemplatives do; indeed, in contemplation we find the most beautiful image of heavenly beatitude, of which it is a sort of anticipation. Both are an ineffable experience of the divine grandeur, although the one is attained in the clarity of immediate vision, the other in the obscurity of loving experience.

Meanwhile, we have understood something of the greatness of contemplation, which introduces us truly into the divine intimacy, and also of the greatness of the contemplative life, which prepares and disposes the soul and leads it to contemplation. It can be concluded, therefore, that it is worth the trouble to prepare oneself with the contemplative life, in order one day to attain contemplation.

But is there really any probability of attaining it? Have we not said, on the contrary, with St. Teresa, that God grants contemplation "to whom He wills, when He wills, and as He wills?" This would seem to indicate a gratuitous contemplative gift and one that depends solely on the divine consent.

It is true that St. Teresa insists on the gratuitousness of contemplation, but to understand her well, we must take into account the whole of her doctrine. She wanted to put us on guard so that we should avoid any claim in our relations with God, as if we could demand from Him the favor of contemplation; this would be to expose ourselves to illusions and delusions. God is master of His supernatural gifts, and He judges how to distribute them to our souls. It would be a real sin of pride to wish to meddle with the divine dispositions. At the same time, St. Teresa affirms, with equal force, that if many souls do not reach contemplation, it is because they do not prepare themselves properly. As a matter of fact, it is possible to prepare oneself for contemplation, and this preparation consists simply in applying oneself to the exercise of prayer and mortification, which constitutes the so-called contemplative life. One who wishes to attain to contemplation, therefore, ought to prepare for it with the contemplative life.

But, as St. Teresa teaches, God invites not just one but all souls to contemplation. He speaks of it in Holy Scripture through the symbol of living water, to which Jesus invites all souls thirsting for God. He also spoke of it to the Samaritan woman, promising her living water that would take away all thirst for the things of this world. He grants it just so that we can esteem how very little all this poor world is worth in comparison with the divine gifts. Teresa elucidates what all who properly prepare themselves will gain from drinking this water.

But, then, how can we reconcile this certainty with the gratuity of the divine gift? Teresa herself gives us the solution: contemplation is an abundant fountain, from which different streams have their source, some small, others large, and some little pools of water. God invites all and will give everyone to drink; but He does not reveal to us from what kind of stream each one of us will be called to drink, nor does He tell us at what moment of our life each of us shall drink.

There are many forms of contemplation. Some are sweet, some arid; some forms attain to great brightness and ineffable sweetness; others are obscure, even painful, but not for that reason are they less useful to the soul. God does not tell us what form of contemplation He reserves for us. He gives it, therefore, as He wills, and when He wills, and likewise to whom He wills, because no one knows whether he is to drink from a great or a small stream; God makes the choice for us. Yes, it is true, He also gives to "whom He wills" but that notwithstanding, some form of contemplation, it would seem, ought never be lacking to the generous soul that can be constant in its preparation.

Hence, God has His part and we have ours. The Lord determines what contemplation He reserves for us; this is His thought of us. But we ought to think about preparing ourselves, because the Lord must not encounter obstacles to the gifts He intends to bestow on us; otherwise we will remain deprived. It is our concern to open the ways to the Lord's gifts, and we do so precisely by living the contemplative life.

We see here what St. John of the Cross is teaching us—namely, the necessary preparation for the soul that desires intimate contemplative union with the Lord. He ardently offers it to us, because in his love for souls and for the divine glory, he desires that this grace be not delayed through our fault; on the contrary he desires that we reach the goal as soon as possible. Now, do we share this holy impatience of the master of the contemplative life?

Union with God

To travel under the guidance of our master, we will begin by raising our gaze and fixing it on our goal — that is, the summit of union with God. While St. John proposes such a goal to us, he will also show us the way to it: through renunciation and prayer.

So, let us enter resolutely on the way of renunciation. He will indicate to us its absolute necessity, and also the way to practice it.

To renunciation, therefore, we should join prayer, which happens to be nourished by renunciation; and here we see that the master's attention is fixed upon prayer. He will teach us to enter the precious enclosure of prayer with the practice of meditation. Then he will show us how from meditation is born a first and humble form of contemplation through a crisis of aridity.

We see the soul, coming out of this crisis, rushing courageously into the way of union, with an assiduous exercise of the theological virtues — that is, of the prayer of faith, accompanied by a total confidence in God and a most pure love.

Again, God makes the soul face another crisis, with the painful but more precious night of the spirit, which will make the soul attain a purity that it could never succeed in acquiring by itself. At last, it is ready for the union that invades it and causes it to live a divinized life. Thus, it can say with St. Paul: "I live, now not I, but Christ lives in me" (see Gal. 2:20).

St. John presents us with a magnificent ideal, but one that nevertheless has its demands; we mean to say that, for its attainment, he exacts effort on our part. But a beautiful, noble soul does not fear fatigue when it is a matter of reaching so exalted a goal. Shall we be able to be numbered among these souls? May the saint obtain this from God for us with his powerful intercession, and let us docilely enroll ourselves in his school. Let us listen to his instructions and then be on our way to the conquest!

It is well worth the effort.

2

The Divine Invitation

In our day, the books of St. John of the Cross have had extraordinary success. Even outside Spain, where the saint is quite a national figure and where editions of his works—always handy and easily obtained—continue to be readily sold, it should also be said that he is an author of worldwide fame. His writings have been translated many times into the principal European languages. In France, there are five versions of them. In Italy, this school has seen two versions and is preparing two others—rather three, and even more it seems. This same thing is happening in every country, which evidently manifests a very great interest in the doctrine of St. John of the Cross.

Nevertheless, there are souls who, after having been drawn by this universal fame, when they have the book in their hands and have read some of its chapters, get tired and put it aside.

Perhaps they experience a sense of dismay when faced with the saint's quite concise and conclusive proof that to attain union one must necessarily pass through the night of total abnegation.

The soul's whole attention is fixed on this night of abnegation, which the explanations of the saint seem to illumine only in order to make one understand better how absolute is the detachment to which he wishes to lead the soul.

Union with God

It looks just like death! Spontaneously the words of the Gospel come to mind: "This is a hard saying" (John 6:60). Yes, we say, this doctrine is hard; it is exacting. I do not feel like embracing it; it is something too great, too heroic for me. Or else: It seems exaggerated to me; it is not possible to live in such frightful annihilation!

Of persons who thus report such impressions of their first meeting with the saint, try to ask what book of the saint they have read. Without doubt, they will answer: *The Ascent of Mount Carmel.*

There you have the key to the mystery!

One should not make one's first acquaintance with the saint through *The Ascent of Mount Carmel*; the first book one ought to take in hand is *The Spiritual Canticle.* I assure you that the impression you receive from it will be very different.

Why?

Because *The Canticle*, from its very first pages, brings to one's notice the magnificent goal to which the saint intends to lead the soul. It is impossible for one who knows a little about the spiritual life not to be enchanted before the prospect of that profound intimacy with God that the saint shows to be attainable even here on earth. Once enamored of that goal that he desires to reach, cost what it may, he will no longer be frightened when he is told of abnegation, renunciation, and the cross.

Obviously great conquests must cost effort and fatigue.

When, on the other hand, one has no idea of the end he wishes to attain, and someone comes to speak to him of the absolute necessity of the total renunciation proposed by the doctrine of St. John of the Cross, it seems to him that this renunciation is the end that the saint proposes. If this were so, there would be no hesitation: I, too, would say to close such a book that proposes such an insane doctrine.

But no, we are not undertaking total renunciation in order to remain in a vacuum; we are not making a place in our soul for nothingness. We renounce created things to find God; we empty the soul of the things of this world to fill it with God. The night of total renunciation is necessary, yes, but in order to attain a more intimate union with the Lord.

Not, indeed, that the saint in *The Ascent* forgets to note that all of his doctrine is intended to teach the soul the way of union, but in this book, especially in the first part, he insists so much on everything that must be removed, that there is the danger — and experience shows it to be a real one — that the soul may forget a little that this work of detachment is not an end in itself but an indispensable means to reach a much higher and more attractive end.

"Through the cross to light!" The cross is only an instrument, a means of salvation and holiness. It is not exact, therefore, to say that St. John of the Cross is the doctor of the cross and renunciation; he is precisely the doctor of the union of love of God.

The Presence of God in Us

From the first to the last pages of *The Spiritual Canticle*, the saint puts before us the soul anxious for union with God.

"Ah, where are you hiding?" it sings in the first stanza of the delightful poem that he will comment on during the whole course of the work. It is the soul's cry of desire for union with God.

This soul, he notes, is the Christian soul. It is not necessarily a consecrated religious soul, a brother or a nun; it is simply the soul that, regenerated by Baptism and reclothed with divine grace, becomes painfully conscious of the potentiality contained in its elevation to the state of a child of God, and desires to see it brought to fulfillment.

I will explain.

Man has need of God. This need finds its first source in our condition as creatures. We exist because God created us and keeps us in existence; not only that, but we have need of Him continually in order to live and to act. Further, our actions are dependent on the Supreme Being, who has to give us the capacity for action even in minute things: without Him, we cannot move even a finger. There are then so many human undertakings before which the serious, prudent man recognizes more clearly than ever his limitations and the uncertainty of success, which frequently depend on conditions over which he cannot exercise his personal influence other than in a very minor capacity. Then especially he feels the need of having recourse to God, of calling upon His omnipotence and providence and humbly asking his Lord to grant him what he does not succeed in procuring himself or procuring it only in a partial or impartial or imperfect way. Man has need of God and of having recourse to Him. If nature already orients us toward the Lord, how much more does divine grace.

We ought never to forget that grace makes us children of God. A man clothed with sanctifying grace belongs to the house of God; he is of the family of God: "You are no longer strangers and sojourners, but you are fellow citizens with the saints and members of the household of God" (Eph. 2:19). He who belongs to the household has a certain right to the goods of the house and to the family inheritance. In the divine family, this inheritance is none other than God Himself. We know this: he who dies in the grace of God will infallibly possess Him eternally in heaven. Grace, therefore, disposes us for the beatific vision; it will make us live in the divine companionship. Grace tends toward this union with God and will fulfill its potentiality only when we truly unite ourselves with Him. That is why there is in the man who lives in the state of grace, a certain inclination, a certain tendency, to live in company with God.

Unfortunately, there are very many Christians who do not cultivate this beautiful inclination, or who smother it under many tendencies and natural impulses that draw them toward creatures and distance them from God. When, instead, a soul seeks to dominate the natural impulses and in this way arrives at a certain interior tranquility resulting from this domination—or rather from a sufficient mastery of itself—this inclination toward God, which was as though hidden and buried under the tumult of the passions, awakens and is easily set free. And here it is that the soul begins to feel the need for God, the need to come close to Him, and there come to the lips the words that the saint puts in the mouth of the enamored soul:

"Ah, where have you hidden yourself?"

We, too, desire to know where He keeps Himself hidden, He with whom we yearn to be united, and for that reason we gladly listen to the saint's reply:

> And so that this thirsty soul may succeed in finding its Spouse and be united with Him in union of love as far as is possible in this life, we may well reply in the name of the Spouse, indicating the most certain place where He may be hidden, in order that the soul may assuredly find Him with the greatest perfection and savor possible.... It is to be noted that the Word, the Son of God, together with the Father and the Holy Spirit, essentially and personally remain hidden in the inmost center of the soul ... and here the good contemplative must seek Him with love.

Here the saint exclaims with emotion in this ardent apostrophe:

> O soul most beautiful among all creatures, who dost long so ardently to know where thy Beloved is so that you may meet Him and be united with Him, at last you have been told that you yourself are the place where He dwells, and the hiding place where He is concealed. Well may you rejoice,

knowing that your whole good, the object of your love, is so close to you, that He dwells in you, or to express it better, you cannot be without Him! (*Spiritual Canticle* I)

This is an important answer and one truly made to bring joy to the soul that wants to attain union with God; therefore, we wish to pause a moment and examine the truth of this solemn affirmation of the saint.

Then, is God truly present in us?

Yes, effectively, God is in us; even more, He can be there in a twofold way: not only with His natural presence, because of His immensity, but also with His supernatural (presence), which is called the divine indwelling.

Let me explain briefly first the one and then the other.

The first presence of God in us, that which is commonly called the presence of immensity, is a consequence of the creative act of God.

We have indicated this above: we exist only through the divine action that, communicating being to us, preserves us in existence, a communication of which God alone is capable. God does not operate as we do — that is, by means of certain faculties that derive from our essence but are distinct from it. God, being simplicity itself, works through His own essence; therefore, where He immediately works, there He is. Hence, since He works in the interior of all creatures, communicating their being, He dwells necessarily in the inmost part of each of them. Since our souls are creatures, God is necessarily present in us; otherwise, if He were not present, He would not operate in us; nor would He communicate existence to us, and we, quite simply, would not be. We would not exist.

Therefore, with all truth St. John can say to the soul: "You cannot be without Him."

That is not all: close to this fundamental presence, in souls clothed with sanctifying grace, there is another that we know only by means of revelation. Jesus has taught us that if a soul loves God supernaturally — and it cannot do so without being in grace — the three Persons of the Most Blessed Trinity will come to it and make their dwelling in it. It is the presence that theologians call "indwelling presence." With this, the three divine Persons become present in a new manner, not simply as the creative cause that preserves and moves all things, but as an object that offers itself to the knowledge and love of the soul, and therefore as an object with which the soul can enter into communication. For that reason, it is said that with this presence, God comes to keep company with the soul and invites it to keep company with Him.

By this special presence of God in the soul, there is a corresponding capacity in it to put itself in a personal relationship with Him. That is because, where there is grace, there are the three theological virtues — faith, hope, and charity — and these supernatural virtues give our souls the capability of establishing an intimate relationship with the Most Holy Trinity. Elevated by faith, our intellect is rendered capable of knowing the Most Holy Trinity, who dwells in us; and our will, corroborated by a confident hope and inclined by charity toward God, the author of all supernatural life, can love Him intimately.

What more is wanting to us to be able to begin, even in this world, a relationship and a union of knowledge and of love with that God who dwells in us?

It will be enough to put into action our theological virtues; and who can say even where this activity may be able to reach, when to the virtues will be united the gifts of the Holy Spirit which, according to theologians, have the property of rendering our knowledge of God in some ways, at least, experiential. Obviously, here indeed we shall meet contemplation.

Union with God

The first presence of God in us, that of immensity, is therefore essential here; but much more precious is the indwelling presence. Let us not forget this, however: it is connected with divine grace, and he who loses grace also loses this precious divine company. This is one of the most disastrous consequences of mortal sin: destroying sanctifying grace in us, it also deprives us of the indwelling of the Most Holy Trinity in our souls!

Seeking the Hidden God

For the soul desirous of union, it is not enough to know where one ought to go to seek God; it also wants to find Him. The soul responds to the Spirit with a new question:

"Granted that He whom I love is within me, why do I not feel Him and do not find Him?"

There is a great difference between having God and being introduced into His divine company, and thus living with Him.

"God is in me," the soul says, "why does He not reveal His presence to me?"

To this, the saint will reply by explaining to us a whole plan of conquest. Listen to why the soul enamored of God, and in whom He dwells, does not feel Him:

> The reason for this is that He is hidden, and you do not hide yourself as He does so that you may find Him and feel Him. He who is looking for a hidden thing should secretly penetrate its hiding place, and when he finds it, he too is hidden as it is. (*Spiritual Canticle* 1, 9)

Yes, it is true: God is within us, but He is hidden, concealed under the accumulation of our too-human preoccupations, all the obstacles to the fulfillment of personal plans for our profit and gain, plans that we want to carry out without taking sufficient account of the divine will and of the rights of others. In our interior, there is too often a whole world of tendencies, of impulses, of very lively passions, that thrust us toward creatures and make us give them our hearts. They make us place our hope in them and seek our comfort in the remembrance of them. So, we live in this superficial world, which occupies us to such a point that it makes us forget that more profound life that we could live but do not live, that truly interior life, in which the soul could be in relation with its God and could end by finding Him. The Lord waits for us, so to speak, in the depth of our souls, but we do not enter this depth, taken up as we are by "our affairs," to which we give all our concern.

Now you see why we do not find Him!

To find Him, we will have to go where He is and escape from that immersion in creatures in which we live. Yes, we must "hide ourselves as He is hidden" and flee our superficial existence to enter a deep interior life, abandoning the more exterior sphere of our human interests, where everything moves around our little ego, to descend into the deeper center of the soul, where it learns to live together with its God.

Listen to the instructions of the saint:

> Since therefore thy beloved Spouse (God) is the treasure hidden in the vineyard of your soul, it is necessary that you, too, forgetting everything and withdrawing from all creatures, hide yourself, until you find Him in the intimate seclusion of your spirit. Here, with the door shut behind you, namely, the will closed to everything, pray in secret to your Father, and then ... in secret you will hear Him and love Him and enjoy Him ... above all that tongue and sense can understand." (*Spiritual Canticle* I, 9)

The saint thus encourages us with the most beautiful promise; he assures us that we will find our God, but at the same time, he insists upon and traces for us a plan of conquest that appears difficult.

Let us examine it more closely.

Renunciation

In substance, the saint is asking two things of us — namely, to make use of the two instruments that we have often heard called the characteristics of the contemplative life. He invites us to renunciation and to earnest entreaties, to mortification and to prayer.

"It is necessary that you, forgetting all your interests and withdrawing from all creatures, hide yourself in the inmost depths of your spirit" (*Spiritual Canticle* I, 9). But perhaps you will say: "The saint asks us to do what we cannot do: forget all our concerns, our business, our duties of state and family. That is not lawful. And then 'withdraw from all creatures.' How is it possible for us who have to live at home, who have dear persons to whose care we have devoted our lives? It would be absurd to want to separate from them! This cannot be the will of God."

And indeed, it is not! We gladly take this occasion to respond promptly to a difficulty that more than once has been held against the saint's doctrine, alleging that it is inhuman, that it asks impossible sacrifices of us, and that therefore his teachings, at the most, can be followed only in solitary cloisters, by persons "buried alive."

He who speaks thus shows that he has not indeed understood the saint's doctrine.

The saint is more "spiritual" than many might think, even in his very doctrine of detachment. Several times in his writings, he has expressly declared that, when he speaks of withdrawing from creatures, he does not mean material withdrawal, as if it were necessary to leave all and go to live as a hermit. But, as he specifies in this same strophe on which we are commenting, it is a question "of leaving all things according to the affection of the will" — that is, of not being attached; and truly this is not the same as not loving it! Let us not forget: God wants us to love creatures, but He does not want us to be attached to them.

There are some affections that are not only legitimate but even holy and positively willed by God; for example, the mutual love of Christian spouses and the love of a mother for her children. Do you think it could be the will of God that a mother not love her children, and that she forget them? On the contrary, if she should do this, she would offend her God, she would commit a grave sin, and St. John of the Cross certainly does not ask us to commit sins.

Then what does he mean to say when he writes of "forgetting creatures" and of "leaving them according to the affection of the will"? He is only telling us to avoid every inordinate affection, every attachment. For the saint, this is the meaning of the word "attachment": love that binds the heart in a way that is not according to the will of God, or in an exaggerated manner. This can be found, and is often found, unfortunately, in the most legitimate affections. Does it not happen at times that a Christian mother cannot resign herself when the Lord asks her for her daughter in order that she may become His spouse in religious life? I do not say that a good woman cannot test her daughter's vocation to see if it is genuine; but once they have all reasonable guarantees on this point, to continue to oppose it, and for fear of the inevitable separation, which doubtless will make the maternal heart bleed, then to insist on "no" is no longer to love according to God.

Let us come down to more humble examples. Suppose there is someone who loves the mountain with its courageous heights, with its bracing air, with its grandiose panorama: splendors of the world that speak with such eloquence of the beauty of the Creator and fill a believing soul with love for Him. Be it so; but he who cannot renounce such an enchanting trip when there is a duty of office or charity to fulfill would show himself undoubtedly attached to it.

When Pier Giorgio Frassati,[4] in the company of friends, showed that he enjoyed a good dish of macaroni, or a savory dish of rice and meat a la Milanese, I could not accuse him of attachment because he could also fast generously when it was a fast day. But one who, to satisfy his taste and appetite, would go beyond the allowed amounts at collation on a fast day or would allow himself to go quite to the excess of gluttony, would evidently be "attached" to such vulgar satisfactions. Often each of us is attached, little or much, to many things, and they are even such attachments that, creating superfluous preoccupations, are not according to God, and which we cannot take with us into His presence, preoccupations that draw us away from Him and shut us up in studied research of personal satisfactions: this is the superficial world that conceals and impedes the interior life and which anyone secular or religious who wishes to attain intimate union with God ought to endeavor to leave.

St. John, therefore, does not ask anything that cannot be done even by a layperson who has many duties of state and family; in reality, it is not a matter of suppressing these, of forgetting them. Quite otherwise, it is a matter of suppressing all excessive and useless attachments, which are too exclusively human and therefore not according to God, and which often accompany the accomplishment of those duties and render their fulfillment less genuine, less sublime, and less noble. In short, St. John teaches us freedom from all that is inferior, by establishing us in a clear, simple life, lived entirely according to the will of God, which is the golden rule of our spiritual perfection.

---

[4] Blessed Pier Giorgio Frassati (1901–1925) devoted his brief life to prayer, good example, and service to the poor. He is the patron saint of young adults.—Ed.

In the hour of prayer, concentrating our attention on God, with whom we wish to speak, we will be led spontaneously to turn our attention away from creatures. One might then be able to see in prayer a fulfillment of the saint's counsel — namely, to forget creatures. But this, too, should be well understood, because we ought not to believe that in prayer one cannot speak to God of those who are the object of our legitimate affections. Certainly, it would be wrong to ask Him to bless an affection not conformed to His will or to satisfy a desire of ours that He does not approve; that would be to ridicule God. But to speak to Him of what we are obliged to do through duty, and hence, according to the indications of His most holy will, which is manifested in the knowledge of what our duties are, is a thing not only legitimate and therefore not blameworthy, but rather quite opportune. This is to treat with our heavenly Father with all that pertains to our life, and to confide to Him all the thoughts of our hearts.

So, we hope, by the above explanation, to have made it understood that the renunciation required by the saint is feasible even by persons who live in the world, and that such renunciation can also be spiritually positive for them, because it is not a matter of material separation from things, but the renunciation of every attachment. There should not be attachments in anyone, not even in one on whom depend the most extensive social duties. A man can be detached from everything not only in domestic life, but also in social and political life, and indeed, everyone could be so. Perhaps in the depth of our hearts we even think: "Would that there were at least some! Our political world would get along better!"

Prayer

The first instrument that the saint suggests to us for attaining the desired encounter with God does not, therefore, seem difficult to employ, but what do we have to say now about the second?

Union with God

After having invited us, by the renunciation of excessive preoccupations regarding created things, to descend into the inmost seclusion of our spirits, where we are in the presence of God, the saint continues: "Here, with the door closed behind you—that is, with the will closed to everything—pray to your Father in secret."

These words of the saint recall the teachings of Jesus with respect to the conditions for good prayer: "When you pray, go into your room and shut the door and pray to your Father who is in secret; and your Father who sees in secret will reward you" (Matt. 6:6).

Jesus, to teach us to pray well, begins by making us withdraw from creatures. St. John of the Cross has only expounded the teachings of Jesus; we see here why his doctrine has the universal character of the gospel doctrine. Let us pay attention, therefore, with faith to what he teaches us regarding prayer.

The search for God comprises a double movement: the first, of separation from creatures; the second, of approach to God. In what way, then, do we approach Him? Listen to the saint's instructions:

> You hear a word full of substance and of inaccessible truth: seek it in faith and in love, without wishing to derive satisfaction from anything, neither enjoying it, nor understanding it, any more than one is obliged to do. (*Canticle* I, 11)

The saint is teaching us pure prayer, prayer in which the soul seeks God and not itself, in that it does not wish to find its own satisfaction, but to give satisfaction to God.

How mean are the concepts we often have of our relations with God! It seems that certain persons pray only to achieve their particular ends, or rather only to succeed, with the help of the Lord, in obtaining what they cannot procure through their own efforts. Then, if they do not quickly obtain what they desire, they become impatient and are almost offended, as if God ought to be benevolently at the service of their human interests. How shallow is our sense of the divine transcendence! We are not the masters; He is. He has created and prepared us for His glory, so that we will be able to procure the accomplishment of His most holy will in everything. That is the reality of things that we sometimes turn upside down, carried away by the impetuosity of our desires.

In St. John of the Cross, we find instead a most profound sense of the divine supereminence. God is, and we, of ourselves, are nothing; we exist only through God. God is the center of the universe, not we. Our perfection and holiness consist in being united to Him, not in becoming persons who have "brought their talent of humanity to the greatest and most harmonious development," as a recent "formula of sanctity" would have us believe. To speak in this way, one must have lost the sense of supernatural realities, which, strictly speaking, are "superhuman" and with which alone man may attain holiness.

It is divine grace that makes saints: it unites us to God, and with its growth, it tends to make us live in God and God in us. This will certainly bring about the harmony of all our faculties, which will all apply themselves in concert, each according to its mode, to procure with their operations "the honor and glory of God." This is simply an effect of holiness, which, as Pope Pius XI of venerated memory one day admirably defined it, is none other than "the Christian life carried out according to the thought and desire of the divine Inventor." Holiness is not anthropocentric; it is theocentric! Holiness is not simply human life; it is Christian life; and that signifies the supernaturalization of human life through the working of divine grace.

In our days, one needs to insist on the divine transcendence, on its absolute elevation above all creatures, even above us human creatures, made by Him and for Him. We ourselves are not to dictate laws to God, but He imposes them on us; and, imposing them, He indicates to us the way of true happiness, the way that leads to union with Him, in which our beatitude consists. We cannot be truly and entirely happy unless we are united to our Principle. True happiness of the present life consists in being united with God even on earth. We will procure this happiness for ourselves by seeking to please our God, by entering into His divine plan, through which we are prepared to render Him honor and glory. The surest way to become happy is to seek to serve God in everything, forgetting ourselves.

It is exactly this disinterested search for God that our saint recommends when he teaches: "Seek Him in faith and in love, without wishing to draw satisfaction from anything."

Oh, how pleasing to the Lord is the prayer of a heart detached from itself that seeks only to please Him, who truly merits this sincere and total homage from His creature!

St. John of the Cross wants us to pray, uniting faith and love. For him, faith is the obscure but secure adhesion to the divine word, which particularly reveals to us the divine transcendence, the supreme grandeur of our God, who is so sublime, and so good, so omnipotent, and also so merciful. Faith places us in the presence of God as He is; not that it makes us see Him, but it makes us believe, and so places our intellect in contact with Him.

Faith is followed by charity, understanding by love. The soul that believes intensely that God is truly God, that He is the Supreme Being to whom we all belong and who merits all our love, will love Him vehemently. Then will be fulfilled in him that which the saint promised here: "The soul will be worthy enough for love to reveal what faith contains in itself" (*Canticle* I, II); thus, faith speaks to us of the divine transcendence, of His supereminence above all creatures. Love will make us delight in it and almost experience it; love will do this in contemplative prayer.

The love of charity, however, is pure benevolence toward God; its purity is the condition of its perfection and of its intensity.

Thus, this love ought to consist in one desire: that of pleasing God, without seeking self-satisfaction. It will not be directed to God in view of His gifts, but only for Him, He meriting to be loved in the highest degree for His infinite lovableness.

Our prayer perhaps is not yet so disinterested, so theocentric, so purely directed toward the divine interests—interests that Jesus, in the Our Father, teaches us to put always in the first place: "Hallowed be Thy name; Thy kingdom come; Thy will be done." We will sometimes be tempted to put in the first place "Give us this day our daily bread," including in this bread all our interests, all our satisfactions. Although God wishes to grant us all that we need from Him (He makes us ask for this precisely), He also wishes that we subordinate our satisfaction to His will and to the fulfillment of the divine plans that, besides, aim only at procuring man's supernatural happiness.

If we do not as yet find ourselves at this moral and spiritual height, nothing on that account hinders us from tending to it. As we possess divine grace, we can legitimately hope that, by maturing within us this grace, with its tendencies to raise us to God and to unite us to Him, we will at last arrive there. Hence, there is also hope for us that prayer may one day become that intense exercise of faith and charity in which "love reveals what faith contains in itself," in which, namely, love lets us enjoy what faith simply teaches, and so communicates the "sense of God": of His uniqueness, of His grandeur, of His transcendence.

If this initial and quasi-experiential perception of God, then, increases in our soul, why should not the saint's promise regarding contact with God present in the soul also be accomplished in us? "Then in the secret place you will feel Him and you will love Him and will enjoy Him ... above all that language and sense can attain" (*Canticle* I, 9).

The Spiritual Canticle, which, from its first lines, places before our eyes an enchanting vision, immense prospects, and a rich, well-balanced doctrinal synthesis, seems, therefore, the book most suitable for fully understanding our saint.

From the beginning of our meditation on the first strophe, we already know where the saint wants to lead us: to the summit of contemplative union with God, where the soul, still on earth, attains a certain possession of Him by feeling Him and enjoying Him.

Not only that, but the saint has put it, I would say, almost before our eyes, so close is this union to us, since God, with whom we are to be united, is already present in the souls—or rather dwelling in them, He offers Himself to our souls to be known and loved.

With knowledge and love, then, we will come near to God. This knowledge and love that are exercised especially in prayer, however, will not develop and will not attain the necessary intensity unless they are nourished in the climate of abnegation and renunciation of creatures.

The two wings with which the soul rises to divine union are mortification and prayer—that is, spoliation and recollection, or, in other words, detachment and prayer. We have already learned their necessity, and we have also understood that these means, indicated by the saint, are within reach of all Christian souls, not only of religious, but also of persons in the world: to these latter also are possible, therefore, the beautiful achievements described by the saint. For that reason, we will gladly follow the saint now in his lesson of total detachment; we will no longer fear his demands. It is worth the pain of imposing on ourselves a little effort to reach so sublime a goal, of embracing a little suffering to attain, even on this earth, so serene a joy. Let us conclude with St. John: "Arise, then, beautiful soul; since you now know that your so-desired Beloved dwells hidden in your heart, endeavor to be well hidden with Him, and in your breast embrace Him and you will feel Him with tenderness of love" (Canticle I, 10).

3

Abnegation

"In search of my love I will go over these mountains and along the rivers, nor will I ever gather flowers" (*Spiritual Canticle* III). It is to the conquest of union with God that the soul's canticle is resolved to rush forward, with all its strength and with all its energies. Its determination is firm, and it cries: "Nor will I ever gather flowers." No, I will never allow myself to be captivated by the satisfaction of creatures. Something of the absolute and heroic resounds in this voice.

But the decision is inspired by love, and love is as "strong as death" (Song of Sol. 8:6). A way despoiled of consolations, bristling with obstacles, and rich in sufferings is shown to the soul, and yet the soul is not afraid. Its ardor urges it on, its hope sustains it, it wants to go to the very end, to union with God, and without losing time, as quickly as possible; not by winding ways, but by the way that ascends directly, straight to the goal. Therefore, it proposes: "Never will I gather flowers."

Is there really a need for such a complete renunciation?

Necessity of Total Spoliation

In *The Ascent of Mount Carmel*, to which we will refer henceforth without fear of alarming the soul, St. John of the Cross has taken care to demonstrate the absolute necessity of total spoliation. His thesis occupies, in his doctrine, so fundamental a place that we believe it opportune to follow the saint in the exposition of his subject.

Spoliation is not sought for itself but is embraced solely in view of union; for that reason, we should deduce the necessity of spoliation from the very nature of union with God. The saint has done this by giving us, in the beginning, a precise notion of this state of union, to which he wishes to lead the soul. We will see that his whole doctrine is dominated by the high concept that he has of the spiritual perfection, or sanctity, to which the soul aspires, and which for him consists in the most intimate union with God that is possible to attain on earth.

This state of union we can consider in different ways. We can, for example, contemplate it in its full integrity, or rather with all the richness that it brings to the soul, with the sweet experiences that it procures, with the most sublime graces of illumination and of divine courtship by which it is accompanied. Thus, we will consider it at the end of the life that we have resolved to go through — that is, after we will have ventured along the various stages of the contemplative way. But for now, conforming to the way of the saint's proceeding, we would like to consider it only in its essential and constituent elements; in other words, in that which is fundamental in the state of union and from which all its complex spiritual riches issue. We will say, therefore, with the saint who defines it for us with all desirable precision:

> The state of union consists in having the soul as regards the will, wholly transformed into the will of God, so that in everything and through everything, that which moves it may be only the divine will. (*Ascent* I, XI, 2)

This splendid formula in which the saint has included everything that is essential in the state of union, or rather holiness, merits to be studied attentively. In it, in fact, we find the keystone of his whole doctrinal edifice.

First, let us take note that, according to the Mystical Doctor, the essence of the state of union is sought in the will. The saint loves to call this union a union of transformation, and we shall quickly see why; but here he declares expressly that this transformation is brought about "with regard to the will." It is not useless to point this out, because there have been, even recently, some who thought they ought to seek the soul's transformation in God by means of the intellect rather than the will, ending up with an interpretation of St. John of the Cross wholly permeated with a philosophical idealism quite far from his thought. We insist, therefore, in saying that the saint is speaking of a transformation according to the will, which results, however, from two facts—one negative, one positive—both being closely connected.

The negative fact consists in the absence, in the will, of every tendency contrary to the will of God that could, for that reason, thrust it in a direction opposite to the will of God. To this absence, however, there is a corresponding presence; the negative element is met by a positive element: in all its operations, the human will is always moved by the divine will. In other words, there is in the soul no tendency at all that is contrary to the divine will, and instead one notes a continuous motion on the part of the divine will.

From that, the saint concludes: "This is the motive for which it may be said that, in this state, from the two wills, one single will is made and this is the will of God, which will is likewise the will of the soul" (*Ascent* I, XI, 3). This, then, is the determining factor in the nature of the transformation: the divine will has become the will of the soul, and the latter has, so to speak, disappeared in the divine will, it is so united with it.

Union with God

How are we to understand this unification? Can that which is human truly *become* divine? Evidently, it would be absurd to understand it as it sounds. So then, what does it mean?

To expound this with clarity, we need to recall briefly the doctrine of St. Thomas Aquinas on the psychology of love, the doctrine by which St. John of the Cross was inspired.

In his works, the Angelic Doctor often speaks of the psychological progress of love, pointing out that, when we love, there rises in the affection, or rather in the will, an inclination toward the object loved. The stronger this inclination becomes, the more it takes possession of the affection and draws us toward the object loved. When such an inclination invades the whole heart, this latter no longer feels any other affection, and lets itself be ruled entirely by the object of its sole love.

By means of this inclination the object loved is, in a certain way, present in the heart and dominates it, and therefore urges it and moves it to act, whence the heart never loses sight of the object loved. In this sense, we speak of a person loved as being "in one's heart." Obviously, we do not mean that the person is physically present there, but that in the heart there is an inclination that urges us to please and to wish that person well. What are we not capable of doing for a person who is dear to us? When we love greatly, we become able to lose sight of our own interests and pleasure in order to gladden the person loved. How generous and forgetful of self does the mother who loves her baby, who has her baby "in her heart," become! The inclination by which she loves the baby urges her to attend to him without respite, to watch over his well-being, to procure his joy and contentment, even though this means having to impose on herself innumerable sacrifices. This is the mystery of love: when we love, the object loved comes spiritually to occupy our hearts with an inclination that urges us toward the loved one, moves us, and makes us constantly act with the loved one in view.

Let us suppose, then, that the object loved is God, or rather, the will of God. In concrete terms, the will of God signifies this: our Lord God requires that His will must be embraced by the little creature He formed, in order that it may glorify Him with full adhesion to His divine will. Let us suppose that a soul, having understood fully this claim of God, has given its whole heart to this most holy will, loving it uniquely and above all. In this case, the divine will also comes to occupy the heart of this creature; it even becomes in it an inclination that moves it to want to be pleasing to the divine will at all times.

In every soul that loves God, such an inclination exists; but many times it is not the only inclination that moves the will. Often, along with God and His will, the soul loves other things very much, without being careful to consider whether they are conformed to this divine will, and sometimes—even often—they are not entirely so. Sometimes, other things are so contrary to the divine will that to love them means to offend our God, and then sin is committed. Other times only a full conformity to the divine will is lacking—that is, while willing a good thing, we remain slack in doing what would be more pleasing to God: a generous impulse is lacking, and then we commit imperfections. In a word, the divine will is not the only object of our love: along with it, and not really conformed to it, we love something else with self-love—that is, with the love that seeks its own satisfaction.

Everything loved in such a way also comes to occupy our hearts; each one gives birth in us to an inclination through which we love it, which drives us to act, moves us, and bears us toward the object loved. Evidently, a will in which, along with the divine will, these other inclinations and impulses exist is not wholly "occupied" by the divine will: it loves God, and it loves creatures. Its love is divided because it not only loves creatures in relation to God but loves them in themselves, seeking in them its personal satisfaction. Then, along with divine love there is love of self; along with the impulse that comes from the divine will, there is that which comes from self-love, from self-will. The soul is moved now by the one and now by the other; here there are two wills.

If the soul renounces loving creatures for themselves and, without allowing itself to be captivated by them, wishes to love only according to the divine will, and controls the love that it bears them in conformity to the will of God, then the soul encloses its love of creatures in the divine will, and it will be able to say that it loves nothing but the divine will. In fact, it loves all the rest *in* God, and *according to* the will of God. In this case, the divine will becomes its only motive.

Then the soul's own will disappears, and the divine will completely dominates; the impulse toward self-satisfaction totally disappears in it to give way to its whole effort in serving the divine pleasure. This soul can repeat the words that Jesus Christ said regarding the will of His Father: "I always do what is pleasing to him" (John 8:29); I seek nothing else, I have no other inclination; in me, there is no other impulse; in me, the divine will alone dominates. My will has disappeared; it is absorbed in in the divine will. Here we have the soul transformed in God according to the will.

This transformation, then, results effectively from two conditions:

1. In the soul, there is no longer anything contrary to the divine will.
2. The will does not love anything "outside" of God, and therefore there is no inclination in it that is not according to the divine will. "In all and for all, that which moves it is the will of God."

The soul that fulfills these two conditions is called by St. John of the Cross a soul transformed in God, a soul that has arrived at transforming union. Quite opportunely, the saint has specified that it is a matter of union of love, since the transformation of which he speaks, we have seen, is effectively accomplished along the direction of love.

A soul transformed in God according to the will is consequently a soul that is moved according to the divine will. That naturally supposes that there are no other movements in it. This is the reason that justifies the fundamental thesis of the saint's doctrine: one does not arrive at union with God except through total spoliation.

Absolute obstacles to transformation in God are all the "attachments," or, as the saint calls them, the "appetites" (that are) not fully regulated.

Let us repeat: it is not that God does not want us to love creatures; on the contrary, He positively commands us to love them, but to love them in Him — namely, in conformity with His most holy will, in the measure established by Him. A creature ought always to be loved with measure, precisely because, being essentially limited, it does not merit more. To say that we love a creature "infinitely," without limit, is a mistake — first, because our love, being a created love, is necessarily limited, but then, too, because a creature is not a being independent of God. It exists only through divine operation, and our love in His regard, in order to be reasonable, ought to take this dependence into consideration. We ought not to love creatures more than God allows, and He does not permit us to give them preference in respect to Him. God ought always to be the one preferred, and every other love of ours ought to be regulated by Him.

But we do not often take entirely into account this duty of regulating our affections according to the divine will, and we set them at once on creatures as soon as we feel the attraction. In many, we find some personal satisfaction; our nature being much inclined to satisfaction, we spontaneously and even deliberately search for the creatures that will procure it for us. So, the "attachments" are hidden, the "appetites" disordered and not moderated in conformity to the divine will.

Union with God

All these attachments are not equally bad, simply because their disorder is not always equally great. Sometimes a person's affection is set on things that God prohibits under pain of losing His friendship, and then the soul that consents commits mortal sin. If it is a matter of things also prohibited but of minor importance, the sin will be venial. If, then, the soul, in acting, lets itself be overcome by its own convenience and shows less generosity than God would like, it will commit an imperfection. In each of these cases, it is always a matter of loving something outside of God, of "attaching oneself" to a creature, of loving what is not solely according to the divine approval. Then it is a sign that in our will there exist other movements besides those that are according to the will of God, with the consequence that the will is not simply transformed in God. It is not a simple will that commands and moves the soul; our own will remains side by side with the divine will. So it does not take much to hinder the transformation of love.

The saint writes:

> Whether the bird be tied with a rope or a thread, it cannot fly; obviously the thread is broken more easily than the rope, but as long as it be not effectively broken, the bird truly cannot fly. (*Ascent* I, XI, 4)

So it is with the soul: so long as it has not renounced the very least attachment, be it still a simple imperfection, the will cannot be transformed into the will of God; the divine will is not its only impulse. Its own will is side by side with the will of God. So long as there are two wills, plainly there cannot be only one!

It therefore becomes evident that, to reach transforming union, the soul has necessarily to embrace total spoliation. To make us understand well how such spoliation — which is born from the desire to attain transformation — is eminently and fundamentally the work of love, the saint did not hesitate to define "love" with spoliation. "To love," he says, "is to despoil oneself for God of all that is not God" (*Ascent* II, V, 7).

Total detachment is the real practical means to establish in us the reign of divine love. The saint's definition indicates the genesis of this reign of love. What must we do, then, to bring about this work of total detachment, the difficulty of which each one quickly guesses?

Rules of Detachment

Some of the saint's pages have had the singular fortune of having been circulated among a wide range of the master's disciples, even before his works were published. These pages are naturally those most typical and most characteristic of his method—those, in a word, in which he teaches the soul what it ought to do practically if it wishes to arrive at this state of union, whose value and riches he so loved to exalt. Before including these golden rules in his *Ascent of Mount Carmel,* he had expounded them in his preaching, and it was in this way that, in the notes of his spiritual daughter, Sister Magdalen of the Holy Spirit, a Carmelite nun of the monastery of Beas, who had listened to his instructions, we find them integrally as they appear in *The Ascent.* It may be that at first they happened to be spread around and even taken out of the book, because Blessed Mary of the Incarnation, who died in Pontoise, France, possessed them at least in the last years of her life. For it was not until the very year of her death that the works of the saint came from the press in Spanish for the first time, and it would be two more years before they would be published in French. Evidently in their original form they roused much interest. Perhaps you may have heard some extract such as this:

> The soul should always be inclined: not to what is easiest, but to what is more difficult; not to what is tastier but to

what is more insipid; not to what is more pleasant, but to what is less pleasant. (*Ascent* I, XIII, 6)

Enough! someone will say. Here we are again at this work of destruction, that takes all the joy out of life, good perhaps for some misanthrope or some heroic hermit, but which will not suit the state of persons who live in the world.

Is that true?

There is no need to misunderstand these passages. Let us put them back into the context out of which they were taken; perhaps in this way they will assume a meaning that will appear acceptable to us.

First of all, let us not forget that in the *Ascent of Mount Carmel*, the saint wishes to lead us very high — even to the state of closest union with God, to the most perfect fulfillment of the aspirations of a soul reclothed with sanctifying grace. And I add immediately: he is well aware that this is a difficult task.

The soul, when it begins to enter upon the spiritual life, finds itself very far from such a state. Ordinarily, at that time, there are disordered attachments and appetites of various kinds within it. These are there in the soul's sensitive nature, which is too accustomed to seeking the satisfaction of the senses and thus inclined to enjoy material pleasures. They are there in its spirit, in which self-love and the complacency of its own excellence are often so great as to make the person tend to make himself almost the center of the world, the center to which everything ought to be directed. Hence, its demands make it impatient, discontented, and basically far from humble.

It will be necessary, then, to purify the sensitive nature and its spirit from evil and imperfect tendencies and inclinations, which are sometimes very strong and deeply rooted in the soul. Great effort is required. One who reflects a little realizes quickly that one cannot reach the coveted goal without energetic exertion, especially if one does not want to lose time and let the most beautiful years of one's life pass by, crawling along in the midst of one's moral deficiencies.

If the work is arduous, that should not discourage us, because we shall not be alone in undertaking it and bringing it to a good end. Considering its loftiness, the saint declares with certainty that it cannot be realized with only the soul's initiative, and that God Himself must necessarily put His hand to it. He teaches that this work is at once active and passive — that man has to act, yes, but he also has to submit to the divine action. He has to undertake the work courageously, but God will come to meet him to lead him to a much greater height than he could reach by himself. Without doubt, it is comforting for the soul to know that it will not be alone in accomplishing this undertaking, but that God will come to its aid, and thus there is truly much greater hope of being able to reach the end.

The soul quickly guesses that a good method for drawing to itself the benevolence of God and the abundant assistance of His grace is certainly that of showing itself generous in undertaking the work; then it is quite disposed to start with zest on the work that belongs to it. It will gladly put forth efforts to enter actively into the night of total purification that is to lead it to union; it will begin by the senses, which are what immerse it most in creatures.

The saint expounds to the soul the most characteristic exercises for entering into this night. They may be reduced to three:

> In the first place, the soul must nurture a lively desire to imitate Christ in everything, conforming itself to His life, which we would do well to reflect on in order to be able to imitate it. (*Ascent* I, XIII, 3)

To make the soul undertake energetically its task of renouncing all human obstacles, the saint begins by introducing it into the sweet company of Jesus Christ, its loving and loved Redeemer. The soul will need to have courage to keep refusing nature the seeking of its satisfaction, because it can happen that the soul will feel very keenly the impulses of its imperfect and perhaps foolish appetites. To say no to self-love and to its "desires," as the saint calls the impulses of self-love, the soul has to have another "anxiety" of love: an ardent love of Christ that will cause it to want to imitate Him. Consequently, it will meditate on the life of Christ to know Him better and to know in what way He acted in life, because His way of acting ought to be the rule of our lives. The whole life of Jesus is summarized in the will of His Father and in doing everything according to His good pleasure and for His glory: "My food is to do the will of Him who sent me"; "I always do what is pleasing to him" (John 4:34; 8:29).

For His love, the soul decides to do the same. Evidently such an exercise is within range of every Christian soul.

No sooner has the soul enamored of Jesus decided to follow Him than it is ready for renunciation. So the saint will then ask it of him. Listen to his second precept:

> In the second place, it ought to renounce any sensitive pleasure whatsoever that is not purely for the honor and glory of God (1 Cor. 10:31).

Many activities are presented to us as attractive, accompanied by the pleasure and satisfaction that entice us to fulfill them. How many actions we perform for the pleasure that we find in them, forgetting to offer them to God, while they ought to be all for His glory, even the humblest action!

"Whether you eat or drink, do all for the glory of God" St. Paul taught the first Christians (see 1 Cor. 10:31).

Is it not true that most of the time we eat and drink hardly thinking of God, and so many times only for the pleasure of it? Such actions are lost for eternity and create and maintain slavery and attachments. To make himself better understood, the saint explains:

> When you are offered the pleasure of hearing something that does not pertain to the service and glory of God, renounce such pleasure and do not seek to hear it. If the delight of seeing something that does not raise the heart to God is offered to you, restrain the nascent desire and refrain from looking at it. (*Ascent* I, XIII, 4)

In other words, whenever we wish to perform our actions not for the glory of God, but to find in them our own satisfaction, let us abstain from them.

Perhaps you will say that often this is not feasible! It is not really possible for us laypeople to abstain from so many pleasant things: we will be acting queerly, and we will make life miserable for others. If a mother of a family were to abstain from so many little innocent and legitimate pleasures inherent to family life for fear of finding pleasure in them, she would fail in her duty of rendering home life peaceful for her husband and children. She would end up by losing the greater in order to find the least.

The saint foresaw the objection; therefore, he added:

> If by reason of necessity or convenience one may not be able to abstain from seeing or hearing, etc., it will be sufficient to endeavor not to enjoy the pleasure of those sensible perceptions. (*Ascent* I, XIII, 4)

In other words, learn to pass over them, without stopping to enjoy them, raising the heart to God, rectifying the intention; and thus, the action will truly be directed to the glory of God.

To mortify self-love in everything and detach ourselves from all things, a good method is not to lose sight of the intention of performing our actions: not because they are greatly pleasing to us — seeking in them, therefore, our own satisfaction — but because they are more pleasing to the Lord. We can also apply this rule to the simplest actions, so that they will come to be effectively directed entirely to the glory of God. Who can say that this is not possible? Like the first rule, the second is applicable to all Christians.

Do not think, however, that it is easy thus continuously to renounce one's pleasure in order to please the Lord. Energy is required for this; and the third rule of the saint is precisely the practice of energy.

The greatest obstacle to our generosity in the service of the Lord and in seeking solely His good pleasure and His glory is our excessive tendency to enjoy, to rejoice in the satisfactions of life. This longing for pleasure thrusts us toward the creatures that immediately offer it to us; unfortunately, too often we let it captivate us. There is need to educate our soul in the direction opposite to this natural inclination; otherwise we will never overcome it.

Thus, we understand better the significance of the famous passages of the saint:

> The soul should endeavor to be inclined, not to what is easiest, but to what is more difficult, not to what is more savory, but to what is more insipid, not to repose, but to labor. (*Ascent* I, XIII, 6)

Note that the saint does not enjoin us to do always the most difficult things; rather, he invites us to nourish the desire and to create in us the inclination and the habit of accomplishment. Yes, there is need to nourish the love for spoliation: "desire, for the love of Christ, to be poor, naked, and empty of all that exists in the world" (*Ascent* I, XIII, 6). The affection ought to be detached from the goods of this world. We need to esteem them for what they are: fragile things that exist today and tomorrow are no more. We need also to be able to do without them when they are torn from us and not let ourselves be discouraged when God permits or wishes that this should happen. These wrenches were daily happenings in the years of war we have experienced; but for noble souls they served to acquire fortitude.

The saint invites us to start out with zest:

> The soul needs to embrace heartily such an exercise of abnegation and virtuous works, training the will in them. (*Ascent* I, XIII, 7)

He is right. If we do not take strong measures against our attachments, we will never conquer them. However, the saint is not inhuman: he remembers that man is a "developing" being and that he cannot bring this about in one fell blow. Therefore, he warns us to proceed with order and discretion. But this discretion ought not to deprive us of energy. Hence, the third rule serves to acquire strength, a strength that will then free us from so much slavery and attachment to our ease and satisfaction and render us prompt for the works that require courage.

Does it still seem to you that St. John of the Cross is asking too much? Our saint is a genius. He also possesses the temperament of an artist, and the artist expresses his intuitions in sensible forms.

One day, he took to his spiritual daughters of the monastery of Beas a drawing that was to become famous in the history of Carmelite spirituality: the design of the "Mount of Perfection"—that is, a graph of the spiritual life. It is a symbolic mountain whose summit, which represents the perfect state of a soul, is graphically represented in a circle. From ancient times, the circle was considered a symbol of perfection. The ascent of the Mount is symbolized by three roads that are directed toward the center of the circle. While the two lateral ones stop halfway, the one in the center, the simple, most direct path, makes its way to the very center of the circle. On this path is written many times: nothing, nothing, nothing. It is the way of complete abnegation. It leads directly to the center of the circle of perfection, where is written the significant sentence: "Here dwells only the honor and glory of God."

By now we know: the soul that lives only for the honor and glory of God is a transformed soul. It moves only by the divine will, which, it is obvious, tends solely to the glory of the Most Holy Trinity. Only the way of total abnegation leads to this.

Whoever desires union with God must desire to travel the path of "nothing."

This union with God is worth the effort of striving on the path of "nothing." In fact, around the central words that express the spiritual attitude of a soul arrived at union, concentrated on God, the saint has arranged in the form of a crown a series of words that indicate the presence of the virtues, of the gifts and fruits of the Holy Spirit in the transformed soul. These signs indicate that the soul enjoys contemplation, that it has entered into intimacy with God and enjoys Him even on earth. To the soul arrived at union is due an earthly recompense, the prelude of the heavenly one. Transforming union creates in the soul a climate in which the gift of contemplation is developed connaturally.

How much is suggested in the saint's drawing!

He reproduced it in an individual drawing for each of his daughters of the Beas monastery, and each kept it in her breviary. It was the best way of keeping the ideal ever present and of nurturing it in the Hours (of the liturgy), in which the soul, on the wings of the sacred psalmody, raised itself to God, desirous of being united to Him. By sketching his design, the saint had rendered an immense service to contemplative souls.

Unfortunately, his design was not kept in its original purity. When the first editors of the saint were making it known, together with his works, they entrusted to a draftsman the care of preparing it for a public presentation. The artist had the unhappy idea of transforming the saint's design into a real mountain decorated with hills, plants, and flowers. He wanted to embellish it, and instead he ruined it. Editors afterward followed the design of the first edition. Thus, the Mount of the saint that was published was for three centuries a deformed Mount.

Ultimately, it was brought back to its original purity, and new editions made it available to the public. We too, like the Carmelites of Beas, can keep it in our prayer books and, contemplating it, can nourish our ideal of union with God. It also repeats to us the saint's great lesson:

> To arrive at intimate union with God one must go by the way of total abnegation.

> One reaches the "all" of God through the "nothing" of creation. "*Nada—todo*; nothing—all."

4

Contemplative Meditation

In the atmosphere of fervor created by the generous practice of mortification, the soul that desires to attain contemplative union with God has to practice meditation—that is to say, mental prayer.

This meditation, according to the teaching of St. John of the Cross, has as its aim to nourish in the soul a determination for abnegation. To teach us to enter on the way of total spoliation that will lead our souls to union with God, he has recommended that we rouse and develop within ourselves a great desire to imitate Christ, the model of perfect abnegation, and to reflect on His life so as to learn from Him how we ought to act. Inspired with love for Christ in affectionate meditation, the soul feels spontaneously impelled to want to live as He did.

This purpose of meditation as proposed by St. John of the Cross is a most important one. But it is, I would say, an "ulterior" one that is reached through a more proximate aim on which we ought to fix our attention: to attain the loving knowledge of God. This purpose makes the meditation of St. John of the Cross an introduction to contemplation.

All the authors who explain the nature of the contemplative life teach that, to render it an effective preparation for contemplation, two practices are necessary: mortification and prayer, particularly mental prayer. Not all authors show with equal clarity in what way meditation can bring the soul close to contemplation. On this, as on many other points, St. John of the Cross is truly a master, although he depends on St. Teresa of Jesus. He is the theologian of Teresian spirituality, into which he introduces a scientific framework that receives its substance from the spiritual Mother of the Carmelite Reform. Even in his doctrine on meditation, St. John of the Cross is completely dependent on St. Teresa. To throw more light on the thought of St. John, therefore, we will not hesitate to have recourse to the teachings of the great Teacher of Carmel.

Concordance with the Doctrine of St. Teresa

In *The Ascent of Mount Carmel*, St. John of the Cross writes:

> The purpose of meditation and of mental discourse on divine things is to derive from them a little loving knowledge of God. (*Ascent* II, XIV, 2)

These are golden words that indicate the particular intonation of meditation according to St. John of the Cross. To understand it well, we need to know the environment in which St. John of the Cross lived, and especially the concepts of St. Teresa by which he was particularly inspired.

In the concept of mental prayer that the Reformer of Carmel had and that she expounded to her daughters, she made clear the affective character she gave to prayer. For her, prayer is "a friendly converse of the soul with God, in which the soul often speaks intimately with Him by whom she knows she is loved."[5] In short, it is an exchange of love: the soul understands that God loves it, and in its turn, it expresses its love to the Lord. It speaks with Him,

---

[5] *The Life of St. Teresa of Avila* VIII, 5.

and it speaks of love, precisely because it has felt the invitation to love. For that reason, St. Teresa has repeated: "Prayer does not consist in thinking much, but in loving much,"[6] insisting thus on the subordination of thought to love. One must, of course, think during prayer—not for the purpose of becoming more learned but rather in order to love the Lord more effectively.

That is why the saint insists: during prayer, do not spend the whole time reasoning, but when, after having spent some time in mental discourse, you are convinced that the Lord loves you, leave reasoning aside and, remaining quiet in the presence of the Lord, start up an affectionate conversation with Him. In this, open your heart with all the desires that you have for Him and for yourself, for His glory and for your needs.

This, for St. Teresa, is the whole substance of mental prayer, and for that reason, it can well be said that, for the great saint, prayer is "a loving conversation with the Lord."

The theologians and spiritual masters of the Carmelite Reform wished to give an organic form to this doctrine of St. Teresa that would render it more apt for being taught to souls. To this end, they distinguished the various parts, or the different moments that prayer presents in its concrete development. They proposed a little method of mental prayer, which has become common in various convents and monasteries of the order and was put together in the first *Instruction of Novices* of the Reform. It has been commented on many times by the first writers of the nascent family of Carmel.

We do not know whether it was St. John of the Cross who organized this method, but there is no doubt that he approved it, because he affixed his signature to the document that authorized the publication of the above-mentioned *Instruction of Novices*, after

[6] Teresa of Avila, *The Interior Castle* IV, I, 7; *The Book of Her Foundations* V, 2.

having "examined and corrected it," as the *History of the Reform* relates. Although we have nothing at all written of him saying that he directly expounded this method—because in his works he has treated of meditation only to show in what way the soul gradually detaches itself from it to go on to contemplation—his first biographer is quite explicit in this regard. In fact, Father Joseph of Jesus Mary Quiroga, who left us a most interesting biography of the saint and was his apologist at a time when his doctrine was meeting with opposition, has stated in a pamphlet the way in which the saint taught his disciples to make meditation. In Father Quiroga's description, we find the whole substance of the little method of prayer that became traditional in the Teresian family.

We have, therefore, all the necessary documents to be able to reconstruct with certainty the teachings of the Mystical Doctor concerning the practice of meditation. We shall see that effectively, for him, all is directed to loving knowledge and affectionate conversation with God in order to prepare the soul for contemplation in the best possible way.

Affective Meditation

To proceed in an ordered way in our exposition, we will follow the outline of meditative prayer proposed by the traditional Carmelite method, which distinguishes seven parts: preparation, reading, meditation, colloquy or conversation, thanksgiving, offering, request. The three last parts are facultative and the two first are introductive, so that every idea of complication is removed from a method that in its substance distinguishes but two parts: meditation and the colloquy or conversation. The first two parts—that is, the preparation and the reading—are destined to put us psychologically in the best disposition to make the meditation and the colloquy well. The three last, which we have called facultative—namely, thanksgiving, offering, and request—are destined to facilitate the prolongation of the conversation with God.

Taking into account the purpose of prayer, one quickly understands the necessity of reading and so-called preparation. If prayer is to end in a loving conversation with the Lord, born and nourished by the consideration of His love for us, this consideration ought to be made on a theme capable of increasing in us the real conviction that God loves us, and that He wants to be loved by us. With reading, we make the choice of a suitable theme, whether we look for it in a book of meditations, or we take it from a favorite spiritual book, or from the liturgy, or from some providential meeting or other.

We quickly understand that preparation is necessary and in what it consists, when we know that the substance and the fulcrum of mental prayer lies in loving conversation with the Lord. One who wishes to speak intimately with another also has to have that person present, because intimate conversation cannot be carried on at a distance. One would have to raise one's voice too much, and then intimacy would disappear. The soul that wishes to converse lovingly with the Lord also has to have Him present, and therefore the preparation of prayer that ends in loving colloquy with God should consist in making contact with Him, in placing oneself in His presence, whether He is sought in the tabernacle of our churches, where Jesus dwells, God and man, or whether we seek Him in the interior sanctuary of our soul, where we know the three divine Persons, who keep us company and invite us to keep company with them, dwell.

Let us suppose, for example, that we want to come to a greater love for our divine Redeemer by means of the consideration of His most sacred Passion, in which He showed so much love for us. We have read in some beautiful commentary on the Holy Gospel the description of the terrible scourging that He endured, and now, at the moment of beginning mental prayer, we recollect ourselves in the presence of the divine Word, adoring Him in our soul, since He really dwells there together with the Father and with the Holy Spirit. We know that Jesus is the second Person of the Most Holy Trinity and that all three divine Persons dwell in us. And so, we have made a good start in beginning our meditation, and Father Quiroga explains to us how St. John of the Cross taught his disciples. We will see here, as in St. Teresa, that consideration sets one on the way to loving colloquy with the Lord.

Consideration or reflection on the mysteries of the Passion is made easier by the representation that we can make of it with the imagination. All of us—some more, some less—can picture to ourselves the scene of the scourging, the description of which we have read in some Gospel commentary. For those who might have difficulty in making this representation, nothing would prevent them from making use of an image, holding it in front of them. But for one who is able to form such an "interior" representation of the mystery, it is well to do so. St. John of the Cross insists, however, that in this work, the soul ought not to spend much time making accurate, detailed representations, and there is no need to do so. Any representation that serves to fix the imagination in some way and facilitates the mental consideration is sufficient. This is necessary to give us more time: the time needed to maintain in our souls a profound effectual conviction that God, the Incarnate Word, loves us and wants to be loved by us.

It seems that St. John of the Cross, as well as St. Teresa, often considered the terrible flagellation scene of the divine Savior, because both of them spoke of it explicitly and recommended a little plan of petitions that seems to have been well known at the time of our saints, an outline that facilitated the meditative consideration: "Who is it who is suffering? What is He suffering? Why is He suffering? In what way does He suffer?" The replies that come spontaneously to these questions are certainly suited to generate in us a deep conviction of God's love for us.

Who is it who is suffering? It is the Son of God, it is the divine Word, the second Person on the Most Holy Trinity, who has put on our human nature and has come into this world just to make reparation for our sins. "For us men and for our salvation he came down from heaven ... became man ... and suffered" (from the *Credo*). He who is suffering is therefore my God, become man for me!

What is He suffering? The horrible torments of the Roman scourging, in which the terrible whips of leather and lead broke the skin, pierced the tender flesh, lacerated it, and in a moment covered the whole body with blood that gushed from innumerable gashes multiplied at every blow.

Why is He suffering? Why does the heavenly Father permit it? Why does the Son of God accept it? It is because He loves us, because with His torments He wants to make reparation for our sins and restore us to the way of salvation and holiness. For this reason, He made Himself a victim for us. He also became a model and an example of patience for us, so that we, too, might be able to suffer something for Him.

In what way does He suffer? Consider this "most patient lamb" that, in the midst of those deadly torments, does not open His mouth and does not even try to avoid the blows of the scourges! He willingly accepts them because He wants to suffer for us, He wants to expiate for us, He wants to give us an example of generosity. Oh, how much love the Son of God has for us!

Do you think perhaps that a soul that thus vividly realizes Christ's love for it does not feel words of love coming spontaneously to its lips, with which it will not also protest that it, too, desires to love, to render love for love, generosity for generosity?

From the pious considerations of the sufferings of Christ, the incarnate Word, there is born in the soul such a need to love in return Him who has loved it so much, that the soul feels constrained to express it, that "it has to tell Him!" And now it begins to speak to the Lord:

> My God, You have loved me so much, and I also want to love You. Oh, how sorry I am to have loved You so little until now! But from now on, O Lord, I want to love You more; I want to devote myself to Your holy love; I want to love You continually and with an ever greater love. Oh, how happy I am that You have opened to me the way to Your heart, the way of progress in love! I do not want to lose my time. I want to make progress incessantly, and I do not want my love to consist only in words. I want to show it to You with deeds: Lord, I want to fulfill Your divine will; I want to be wholly at Your service!

The soul can formulate these expressions of love in a thousand ways, even continuously, pronouncing them likewise with the lips.

This is not, however, the only way of manifesting our love. As long as the sensibility has a large share in the spiritual life and gives the soul some of its particular tonality, it will be easy for the expressions to be frequent, formulated with words, and also pronounced with the voice.

When instead — and this happens spontaneously with progress in the spiritual life — the will dominates over the sensibility, although love continues to have some resonance in the sensible heart, the manifestation of love becomes less impetuous and less tumultuous. It gains in depth what it loses in frequency and in exteriority. The soul then exhibits its love more tranquilly, but the movement of its will toward the Lord is more decisive and earnest. It remains gazing at God, gazing at the Incarnate Word, whose love for it is now better known. At this time, it does not make further mental discourses; it no longer "searches" with reflections; it no longer feels the need; it has "understood" and now savors the fruit of its searching in that intuitive gaze with which it contemplates Christ, who suffers for love and invites us to love. As Father Quiroga explains, expounding the teaching of our saint, "it remains devotedly attentive to God in an act of love."

It has attained, at least for a few moments, a kind of loving attention to God, in which, without a multiplicity of acts, with great simplicity, but also with real depth, it applies itself to God, in a quiet but intense movement of love.

Then especially, notes Father Quiroga, prayer becomes a conversation with God; not only does the soul speak with Him, but God speaks with the soul. It is not that He makes His voice sensibly heard, but He gives the soul that light by which it perceives more of the greatness of God and how He merits to be loved above all things. He also gives it the loving motion with which He aids the soul to love.

This quiet, tranquil colloquy with God, in which the will is profoundly moved toward Him, a colloquy sustained by a recollected gaze on His divine amiability, is for St. John of the Cross the true goal and end of prayer. He alluded to this when he wrote:

> The scope of meditation on divine things is to derive from it a little loving knowledge of God. (*Ascent* II, XIV, 2)

Connection with Practical Life

Mental prayer does not end here, or at least it ought not to end here. To have its full efficacy in our spiritual life, it should have a practical impact on the way we live, introducing good, generous habits of practicing virtues and abnegation. Let us remember that St. John of the Cross recommended that we nourish our will with total abnegation by means of meditation on the example of Christ, whom love urges us to imitate.

Union with God

In the consideration of His terrible flagellation, while we have nurtured our love for Christ, we have also admired His patience, His generosity in embracing sufferings for love of us. That love urges us "to wish to live as He did," so now is the moment to draw from it practical resolutions of self-denial. The last part of prayer is meant to determine and strengthen these practical resolutions.

The second part of mental prayer ought not necessarily be extended. We have called it "facultative," precisely because it does not always present the same development and is sometimes reduced to recalling, with renewed vigor, a practical resolution that we have already formulated many times in the preceding periods of prayer. At the end of a period of prayer passed almost entirely in speaking lovingly with the Lord of our desire truly to love Him, we renew this resolution by way of practical conclusion, by turning then to our daily duties, in which we will probably find abundant occasions to carry out our resolutions. When the soul once knows well what the Lord is really asking of it and when it possesses a certain facility in conversing lovingly with the Lord, there is no objection whatever in proceeding even habitually in this way.

Not all souls have the same facility, especially in the beginning. Some, if they should want to stop speaking only of love with the Lord, would quickly find themselves in idleness or in a kind of boredom. They weary of repeating always the same things, although it may be true that the Lord does not tire of hearing us repeat that we love Him and want to love Him. Here there is a difficulty on the part of the soul. To remain attentive, at times it needs to find a little variety, and it will be able to prolong its affectionate conversation with the Lord more easily when it has several things to tell Him.

It is to aid it in this that the Teresian method, approved by St. John of the Cross, offers it the three last parts, called thanksgiving, offering, and request. While it thus continues speaking with the Lord, the soul will also have the most beautiful occasions, as stimulus to a more fervent practice of abnegation, to make use of the more intense love that it has drawn from meditation on the most holy Passion of Christ.

After having lovingly contemplated the Lord suffering for our love, and having multiplied its words of affection, the soul will be able to feel drawn spontaneously to express its gratitude to the Lord and thus to add acts of thanksgiving to those of love.

Our gratitude will not be limited to thanking Jesus for having wanted to suffer so much for us but will also serve to manifest our gratitude for the fruits we have received from His sacred Passion: the immense fortune of possessing the grace of God, of being Christians, of being children of God, of being able to live in contact with God present in our soul. All of these things have been merited for us by Jesus Christ. For these we can thank Him, not only for ourselves but also for so many persons dear to us who enjoy these same benefits of His.

A heart that is noble and moved to gratitude will be able to take delight for a long time. A noble heart, precisely because it knows it has received much, feels that it ought to make a return. For this reason, the oblation and the offering will spontaneously be born from its gratitude. This is the time to form our resolutions, or to go back over them to strengthen the will to observe them. Not content to tell the Lord in a general way that we want to serve Him, we will get down to particulars, to our present needs.

The needs of a soul that desires union with God are great! From how many things it has to detach itself, and how much energy it has to acquire to go to "not what is easiest, but to what is more difficult, not to what is pleasurable, but to that which is disgusting," in order to embrace an austere mortification that will enable it to free itself from every attachment. The soul well understands how much Jesus has loved it, how much He suffered for it, since for it He despoiled Himself of everything, of comfort, of well-being, of life. Will it not, therefore, have the courage to make some renunciation for Jesus? Oh, yes! It will endeavor continually to purify its intentions. It will want to do everything in the way most pleasing to Jesus and to the heavenly Father. It will desire to live, no longer for itself but for the honor and glory of God!

The soul will decide, therefore, to remove the obstacles that hold it entangled: the attachment to a pleasure that is not according to the will of God, to an excessively sensible satisfaction; the attachment to a created object that comes from an excessive search for ease; from self-love, on account of which it is intolerable of others' defects, often failing in charity toward the neighbor with clashes, rudeness, or complaints.

"Jesus, who loves me so much," it will say, "does not want all that! He has given me the example of total renunciation; I do not want His sufferings for my soul to be in vain. Just because I want to return so much love, I want to renounce myself, to sanctify myself, and to attain perfect union with Him!"

Nevertheless, the soul, also through experience, realizes its weakness and knows that, to become holy, it is not enough to make good resolutions. It needs to carry them out faithfully, and that is not easy. On the contrary, it is a question of supernatural matters, or rather of the life of grace. It does not forget that Jesus has taught: "Apart from me you can do nothing" (John 15:5). To make progress in the life of holiness, it has need of divine aid. This it has to ask for. The Lord has told us: "Ask and you shall receive; knock and it shall be opened to you" (see Matt. 7:7).

So, the soul knocks at the door of the Lord and begs: "Lord, help me! Without you, I can do nothing." Remembering its past weakness, the occasions of temptations, it insists: "Lord, strengthen my soul! And lead us not into temptation" (see Matt. 6:13).

The soul asks for itself, but charity urges it to ask for others also: for the souls in its care, for those most in need, for sinners, for the dying, for the dead, for priests, for its country, for the Church. There are so many things to ask the Lord, and in this atmosphere of love that permeates it and in which it feels itself loved by God, the soul is therefore trustful from speaking to the Lord with the most intimate confidence, sure of His efficacious help.

The Contemplative Gaze of the Soul

All this loving conversation of thanksgiving, offering, and requests will consequently prepare the soul for an effective life of love in which love will show itself with generous actions. It will also serve to reinforce in the soul that loving attention to God, which is the immediate end of meditation, that intimate conversation with the Incarnate Word, upon whom the soul gazes with an intellectual regard enriched by the concepts on which it has meditated. It has understood God's love for us and turns with all the strength of its will, determining to love Him truly. From the loving knowledge of God it has come to some practical resolutions, which it knows it needs, and renders those resolutions more efficacious by drawing profit from the gaze of love that rises to Him from its heart. On the other hand, the same efforts that the soul makes to be more generous, nourish its love; they kindle the heart all the more and make it feel an intimate desire to remain in this loving divine company.

The real center of prayer, therefore, is the exercise of the loving knowledge of God and conversation with Him, sustained by the affectionate gaze of the soul penetrated by love.

St. John of the Cross has determined the double scope of mental prayer: to arrive at an intimate conversation with God—in which the soul speaks to the Lord and God also speaks to the soul—and then to sustain the will by total abnegation. As we have seen, the second aim is reached through the first, and the same resolve of giving itself generously to the practice of abnegation aids the soul to declare its love to the Lord, with a stronger and sincerer will. Speaking then of the end of mental prayer, the saint indicates it admirably:

> The scope of meditation on divine things is to derive from it a little loving knowledge. (*Ascent* II, XIV, 2)

We know what the saint means by this "loving knowledge": it is that rather quiet and restful spiritual attitude to which the soul attains at the end of attentive consideration of a divine mystery, consideration by means of which it feels itself moved to love its God more than it has loved Him.

We call this attitude "rather quiet and restful," because at this time, reasoning ceases in order to give place to a simple, affectionate regard to the Lord, with whose goodness the preceding meditation has made it better acquainted. Not only that, but perhaps—and this is especially verified in a soul already accustomed to meditating—the colloquy, which at that time begins with the Lord, is also very tranquil and does not multiply words. It therefore comes little by little "to have loving companionship with the Lord," more with a simple movement of the heart, or of the will, than with formulated expressions. To this silent language of the soul that looks affectionately at God, He responds with His grace, which enlightens it and draws it to Himself.

In *The Ascent of Mount Carmel*, St. John of the Cross has explained that these acts of loving knowledge prepare the soul for contemplation, precisely because they accustom it, a little at a time, to gaze at Him with a regard full of love. The meditation well made, explains the saint, often leads the soul to these happy moments of loving conversation with God. When multiplied, these passing and frequent acts create little by little in the soul a habit of remaining with God, occupied only in gazing lovingly at Him. The soul thus acquires, in a certain way, a contemplative waiting, at least as far as it is in its power. It comes to accustom itself psychologically to the contemplative gaze.

To make progress, the soul will also need the intervention of the Lord, and He, in fact, will come to meet the soul to fulfill its aspirations. Nevertheless, He comes to meet the soul in a way that many are far from expecting—that is, by producing a crisis in the soul, the painful crisis of aridity. This will be the Lord's work, and we shall make a study of it in the following chapter. In the meantime, we have seen in what way the soul does its part, preparing itself for contemplation with loving meditation, which, for that reason, we have called "contemplative" meditation.

5

Aridity

"If the soul is seeking God, its Lord is seeking it much more" (*Living Flame of Love* III, 28). These words of the Mystical Doctor in his *Living Flame of Love* are certainly very encouraging. They repeat in a moving way the consoling doctrine — which is not exclusively the saint's but is formulated by him with such great clarity — that our sanctification does not result just from our activity, but is principally the Lord's work; it is work that we have to endure, accept, and further. Not all souls understand these words well, and they believe too easily that this approach of God to the soul, that this coming to meet us and seeking our heart, signifies overwhelming us with consolations and comforts.

They have not noted that St. John of the Cross wrote these words with respect to the appearance in the spiritual life of a phenomenon just the opposite of comforting — namely, of aridity, into which so often, after a period of special euphoria, or interior serenity and contentment, the soul that has put itself generously at the service of God, suddenly sees itself introduced with great suffering and temptations to discouragement.

Nevertheless, if we reflect a little, it should not surprise us that the Lord comes to meet us not with sweetness but with trial. In fact, we have understood that total union with God, transformation in

Him, requires the absolute purification of the soul from every attachment, a purification so complete that, according to the thought of the saint, the soul is not capable of bearing it to the end with only its personal strength. It is necessary that God put His hands to the work, and He comes to tear away from us what we ourselves shall not succeed in completely freeing ourselves from. The expedients of our self-love are so subtle, and drive us to such hidden assents, that we are not capable either of unmasking them all, or of eliminating them completely; they contaminate our works and even our prayer! We want to pray, yes, to please God; but when everything goes well, it is so easy for us to seek ourselves a little also, desiring consolations and comforts in which we find satisfaction and pleasure.

God wants to free from this weakness and puerility the souls that He sees are truly determined to love Him, and that show the reality of their decision particularly by their application to the practice of renunciation and of mental prayer. These souls are generous with the Lord, and He who is never lacking in generosity will come to meet them to introduce them to a higher plane of spiritual life; precisely for this reason does He have them fall into aridity.

The Nature of Aridity

By "aridity" is meant the suppression of the pleasure that is often experienced in the spiritual life, a suppression that happens particularly in prayer that becomes obscure and cold.

When a soul is converted to God—and we mean here by "conversion" not only the rising from sin to the life of grace but also the decision made by a good soul that may be a little aimless and distracted to give itself to the life of perfection—it usually experiences at the beginning a certain joy and some pleasure.

Aridity

It is a psychological law that when a man understands that he possesses a great good, joy springs from his spirit. When the soul that is converted to a more perfect life compares its present life with its preceding one, it sees that, while before it used to pass its time in so many vanities and frivolities of the life of the world, now instead it serves the Lord and makes itself useful to other souls and to the Church, with its works of prayer and charity. Seeing that it has thus acquired a great good that it did not possess before, it cannot do less than experience a certain joy from it, which sustains it and gives a tone of serenity and joy to its psychic life.

Similarly, it experiences much comfort in prayer, in which it is easy for it to remain with the Lord. Hardly does it begin to pray than it is quickly presented with many good thoughts that stimulate its will and move its heart, while words of love spring spontaneously to its lips. It speaks with the Lord with tenderness and sweetness and experiences much consolation.

For this reason, the practice of mental prayer is really not burdensome! The soul makes it willingly, evidently with the intention of pleasing the Lord; but can we exclude that it may also perhaps be attracted by the satisfaction that it finds therein? It is here that its weakness easily enters into play — namely, the search for personal satisfaction that contaminates in some way its purity of intention. Then the Lord, who wants to free the soul from such misery, makes it fall into aridity.

The soul, accustomed to remain in comforting meditation and in sweet colloquies with the Lord, one day finds that its situation is completely changed. Although it may prepare itself in the usual way and willingly betakes itself to church, when it puts itself in the presence of God to begin its prayer, it seems not to succeed in finding Him and it cannot make any contact with Him at all. It recalls to mind the subject of its reading and the point of its meditation, which it would like to ponder deeply, but it experiences difficulty in understanding the thought. It seems to have become incapable of penetrating its sense: the concepts vanish, they fade away, and the mind remains almost in a void; the imagination at times becomes agitated and turbulent, thus adding the torment of distractions.

Neither does the affection find itself in better condition. When the soul attempts to express its love to the Lord, instead of the usual sweetness, it finds in itself only hardness, and it can only protest its love with a pure act of the will, which has no resonance at all in the sensible affections. It seems that the spring flowering has been changed into a dark, hard winter.

Although a little alarmed, the soul takes courage thinking: "Patience! Tomorrow it will go better." But the next day, even after preparing itself with great care, it meets the same difficulty and thus again the following day. What has happened? Perhaps its whole spiritual life, which seemed to promise so much good and for which it nourished such beautiful hopes, has gone up in smoke. Desolate, it goes for an interview with its spiritual director and explains its case.

"Have patience," he replies. "Don't worry. It is nothing; it is a matter of aridity."

Causes of Aridity

On the subject of aridity, St. John of the Cross has dealt with particular mastery. It is one of the principal points of his doctrine that some, not understanding it, find discouraging in its austerity. Here the saint instead reveals himself a great consoler of the tried soul because he makes it understand that the trial hides a great grace and the apparent regression signifies the call to a higher stage of spiritual life. When the aridity is sent from the Lord, it becomes the means of certain progress.

But does it really come from the Lord?

Aridity

This is the first question that we must examine, because aridity can manifest itself in the soul under the influence of different causes, some of which are not good. The soul, to remain tranquil, has to make sure that such causes have nothing to do with its case. To aid it in this examination St. John of the Cross gives it "three signs" by which it can recognize the purifying aridity sent by the Lord.

These famous three signs were not discovered by the saint; they already existed in ancient spiritual tradition, and they are also found in the so-called *Institutions* of Johannes Tauler. But in the doctrine of our saint, they take on a special importance because they came from him after profound study. They were well used in two instances to characterize the delicate passage of the soul from meditation to contemplation, and from an interior life—still quite dependent on sensibility—to a life more purely spiritual. The saint makes use of them in *The Ascent of Mount Carmel* to confirm, in its new way and in its new way of dealing with the Lord, the soul that has already passed through the crisis of aridity. Then, in *The Dark Night*, he makes use of them to identify the divine origin of the crisis itself. Consequently, these signs, substantially identical, present some accidental differences in the two places cited.

In the present case, the saint makes use of these signs to exclude the influence of the other causes, different from the divine one, which alone gives the trial a reassuring, beneficial character. The other possible causes of aridity make of it a natural phenomenon and are anything but desirable: one's faults; tepidity; psychophysical indispositions; physical anxieties—namely, those that affect our psychic faculty and hinder its normal operation. The first sign is destined to exclude the effect caused by one's faults.

Unfortunately, the soul sometimes falls into aridity through its own fault. It can happen that, after a certain time of application to the spiritual life, the soul becomes unfaithful and proves inconstant. I do not mean to speak here of some moment of unexpected weakness, after which the soul quickly repents and from which it rises with a will more determined than ever to apply itself to virtue. No, I am speaking of those voluntary faults by which the soul returns, with a certain deliberation to the evil or the imperfection that it decided to combat in order to follow the Lord in the way of total abnegation.

It had already resolved to seek its own satisfaction no longer and, therefore, to mortify its appetites so as not to attach itself to anything; but here it has grown weary and, finding it too hard continually to say no to nature and yes only to the Lord, it begins to say yes also to the desire for pleasure, and although it feels that this is not pleasing to the Lord, it does not have the courage to refuse. In the beginning, it was perhaps a matter of a small thing: for example, giving oneself a little more freedom in talking, though one had resolved to watch the tongue carefully so as not to fail completely in patience, in charity, in humility; or to be exactly punctual in all one's duties in order to take nothing from one's exercises of piety. The soul succeeded in restraining self-love by means of a faithful exercise of continual mortification, and thus went so far as to lull it a little; but dead it was not. It is made of strong fiber and when it seems soothed, if given barely a little food, it wakens at once and recovers its vigor, making its demands felt; and thus, the soul begins to slip.

Oh, if good souls that have decided to give themselves wholly to the Lord could know the mistake they are making by deliberately turning back, like a dog to his vomit, to the little satisfactions in which it once took pleasure, how careful they would be not to commit such inconsistencies anymore! These they pay for dearly because the desire to enjoy, awakened, tries to get the upper hand, and then we see that just for the sake of enjoyment, the soul does not refuse even to sin venially. It is easy to commit a venial sin by surprise, so much so that it even happens at times to good souls, but if they regret it immediately, they rise again and are more watchful than ever not to fall again. On the contrary, venial sin can be committed with deliberation, with the eyes open; one is well aware that the Lord does not want this action, this gesture, that word, and yet one does it just the same. St. John of the Cross has noted well that, when a soul commits such failings, it is wounded by them, and these blows awaken in it the attachment to creatures. It begins to be tempted immoderately by them, just because they come to occupy its heart again. The soul, finding itself once more in search of created things, can no longer feel the same desire to love the Lord, and so falls into aridity. This certainly is not the aridity sent by God.

Instead, the soul to which the saint is here referring, although falling by surprise into some fault, remains firm in its resolve to renounce everything for the Lord and to give itself wholly to Him.

Therefore, the first sign by which the soul will be able to recognize that its aridity does not come from failings that it may have committed, but from the Lord, is this: "In the same way in which it cannot find pleasure or consolation in the things of God, so it finds none in creatures." The soul to whom God sends aridity no longer feels the joy of being with Him but cannot tell itself for that reason that it should return to creatures, because it remains firm in its decision to detach its heart from them. Hence, it finds no pleasure in prayer, nor does it find enjoyment in creatures. If, instead, it should fall into aridity from being unfaithful and from having returned to created things, it would feel itself very inclined to them and disposed to enjoy them.

The sad effect of repeated voluntary faults is so-called tepidity, which makes the soul lose every impetus in the service of God, having fallen into a kind of convenient apathy. It no longer has concern for the holy love of God. This is not to be wondered at. Voluntary venial sin, as theology teaches, has the property of diminishing the fervor of divine love, the impetus toward God, so connatural to the love of charity. When fervor continually diminishes, it finally disappears altogether. With deliberate venial sin, the soul goes contrary to the will of the Lord, while fervor urges it to want to do the will of God. These two movements are contrary to each other, and when venial sin is multiplied, its influence has the upper hand, and there we have the source of tepidity. It is a dangerous state, because a tepid soul has little strength to resist evil, and if some great temptations should come, there is danger that it would lack the courage and strength necessary to resist them.

The catechism logically teaches that when venial sin is deliberate, it prepares the soul for greater falls. If venial sin is multiplied, it maintains the soul in apathy with regard to God, and in indifference with regard to His service. It is evident that a tepid soul is an arid soul, but its aridity does not manifest the second sign that has been indicated by St. John of the Cross: "Ordinarily it is occupied in the remembrance of God with solicitude and painful preoccupation, thinking that it is not serving the Lord" (*Dark Night* I, IX, 3).

No, a soul that has fallen into tepidity does not experience the painful preoccupation caused by the fear of not serving the Lord; it has become indifferent. If the soul remains anxious in its service of the Lord, it is a manifest sign that its aridity is not caused by tepidity. The second cause is therefore excluded.

The third cause of natural aridity is brought about by the effect of psychophysical indispositions, which the saint, in the terminology of his time, indicates under the name of "melancholy humor" or other similar terms. In the latter we can include all those indispositions, light in themselves, but which cause dullness and boredom, that keep us hindered in the use of our psychic powers — for example, a great fatigue, unusual torpor caused by bad digestion, an almost unconquerable sleepiness, a heavy cold that enervates the brain, suffocating heat: all indispositions

basically physical, which, however, have a reflex in the psychi-
cal life, because they render the soul more or less incapable of
operating with its powers.

Let us suppose that after a very hot summer night in which
you slept little, because the atmosphere was so oppressive, you get
to church early in the morning with the sincere determination to
pray, yes, but with your eyes heavy with sleep. Inevitably during
your prayer, you will feel the inclination to sleep. At that time, you
will certainly feel little devotion. Let us suppose, however, that you
fight generously to stay awake (because if you let yourself go, you
will certainly fall asleep). If, then, you fight, you should not think
that you have not made your prayer well. On the contrary, more
than *telling* the Lord that you love Him, you *show* him, because to
struggle against sleep is quite a hard thing. Naturally, your prayer
will not be very consoling; doubtless you will experience great
aridity. But take note, when you have had a good rest the following
night, you will once more turn easily to making prayer, and you
will see aridity disappear.

That will be the case, more or less, with the different physical
causes that momentarily disturb the readiness of our faculties.
They are difficulties that come and go; hence, the aridity they
cause is transitory. Not so with the purifying aridity caused by the
Lord. This is established in the soul. At first, yes, it can present
some fluctuations and days of greater or lesser intensity; but still,
through those highs and lows, it progressively invades the whole
soul and renders meditation downright impossible.

We see, then, that the third sign given by St. John of the Cross
"consists in not being able any longer to meditate or converse as
before using the faculty of the imagination, notwithstanding the
soul's efforts." The saint notes opportunely that this impossibility
becomes continuous little by little and establishes the soul in a
state of real impotence.

Union with God

A Divine Favor

We have been marvelously helped in excluding the culpable or natural causes of aridity and therefore in ascertaining if our aridity comes from the Lord. But the saint is not satisfied with this, and he lets us know that this trial also contains, hidden in itself, a great divine favor. He is not one of those who, when faced with a difficulty, content themselves with saying, "Have patience!" He will indicate to us how we are to comport ourselves in this aridity in order to profit from the gift that the Lord offers us and to second the work that God is bringing about in us.

Explaining the Lord's intention in sending us purifying aridity, the saint declares that by means of this trial, God makes the soul pass from meditation to contemplation. Even more, this latter begins to be communicated to the soul in the very midst of aridity.

Are we to be astonished? How? At this point to speak of contemplation with respect to aridity? The latter seems to us to be far from every form of prayer. We see our spiritual life going up in smoke, and you want to make us believe that God is granting us one of His most sublime gifts?

First, let us try to understand the saint's affirmation in its proper relations. We should remember that to enjoy contemplation is not the same as going into ecstasy. It is simply beginning to know God no longer just with the intellect, but through the experience of love—experience that does not communicate new ideas of God to us, but that gives us the "sense" of His greatness. Many persons imagine contemplation to be something extraordinary, confounding it with visions and revelations, and believe that it makes one see clearly into divine mysteries. I repeat that it is not a question of this, but of a new knowledge of God, which is rather of an affective and experiential nature, in which the principal part is held by love that forcefully attaches itself to the divine object and thus gets from it a particular "sense," a certain experience of God. St.

John of the Cross explains how such knowledge of God begins to be formed in the soul in the midst of this aridity.

Let us return to the signs of purgative aridity that he has mentioned so as to distinguish it from the aridities harmful to the soul.

We have considered these signs in their negative function, concerning the exclusion of undesirable causes. Now let us look at them, especially the second and third, in their positive and constructive meaning.

The second sign presents us with the soul that is all-solicitous for the service of God, and that therefore, in the midst of its aridity, keeps a continual remembrance of Him. This remembrance is as if wrapped in anxiety from the fear that the soul has of not serving its Lord better, of not loving Him anymore. The most beautiful proof that it really does love Him is the deep pain that it feels in the fear of not loving Him. This pain does not leave it. It is as though installed within it and keeps it occupied and preoccupied: yes, preoccupied with not serving that God, who—it is ever more convinced of it, and this deep conviction augments its pain—merits infinitely to be loved. This pain, which torments it, and the esteem of God, from which it proceeds, are the manifestations of a hidden sense of the greatness of God, a greatness not known just now by means of reasonings, because here there are none, but of which the soul is "aware," because it finds itself deeply in love with Him as with its true "all."

While this second sign reveals a new manner of occupying oneself with God, consisting in that anguish of love itself, the third sign concerns the absence of conceptual knowledge; the soul finds itself unable to go to God by its customary way of discursive thought. It no longer succeeds in considering, in reflecting, in examining thoroughly; on the contrary, it experiences tedium and trouble in it. It no longer feels inclined to follow this way, which besides has just been shut to it. It is not tranquil because it still has not understood that a new way has been opened to it, that of love, with which it makes better progress than with the understanding.

If, then, contemplation is simply the knowledge of God that proceeds from love and produces the "sense" of God and of His grandeur, without the soul forming any precise concepts of Him, we will not have any more difficulty in admitting the saint's affirmation — namely, that contemplation begins to be granted to the soul in the midst of aridity. Happy then that soul! But then why is it disturbed?

Conduct of the Soul

In truth, the saint teaches the soul not to be disturbed and instead to surrender to God, who has begun to work in it, so that He may find no obstacle to His action.

It happens more often that the soul, in its anguish and in the fear of having lost its spiritual life, which seemed to flourish so perfectly when meditation was easy for it, might want to return to it by force. Sometimes it even happens that some director not sufficiently instructed in the spiritual life believes that methodical meditation is the only safe way, which he does not want to allow the soul to leave. It is understandable, then, that the poor little soul wants to take up this meditation again, cost what it may. But the hand of the Lord cannot be forced, and if He renders the soul unable to meditate just because He wants to put it on another road, there is really no hope that it can succeed in turning back. Therefore, such a way of acting, instead of pacifying the soul, causes it greater anxiety.

Quite different is the teaching of the master of contemplative souls. To the soul that, by means of the three signs, has recognized its aridity to be purifying aridity, he says, of course, that it should leave meditation aside and not force itself any more. The Lord no longer expects that from it, but He wants it on another road.

What, then, should it do?

It should learn to be content to remain in the presence of the Lord, attending to Him simply with a regard full of love. It should remain there to keep Him company, satisfied to speak some words of love to Him from time to time. Little by little, it will become accustomed to make its prayer in this way. Then it will become aware of being in contact with Him in a way, in essence, that is better than the former.

"But I do not know how to love the Lord anymore!"

Do not believe it! It is true, you do not love more sensibly than you did at first, when your heart was moved at the thought of God's love for you. But remember that the love of supernatural charity is not a sensible love; it is a love of the will, which it is not necessary to feel. It consists only in an interior decision of the will, with which the soul gives God preference above all creatures and wants to consecrate itself wholly to His service. This love is there in you, and this is true love, the love that leads to the "sense of God."

More than that, St. John of the Cross believes that, with the crisis of aridity, there begins to be born in the soul what he calls "infused love." With this love, the soul not only thrusts its will toward God, protesting that it wants to love Him, but also happens to be secretly drawn to God. In such a state, the soul's love greatly increases, and it progresses rapidly in the ways of the spirit. While from one side it is pushed on, from the other side it is drawn, so it travels quickly!

Benefits

For that reason the saint greatly enlarges on the advantages that the "night of aridity," as he calls it, into which God has introduced the soul, produces.

Union with God

This night has caused obscurity and painful anguish in the soul, but it has also given it many spiritual benefits — first, a great feeling of its littleness and misery. Now the soul knows, through experience, that without the Lord it can do nothing, and this establishes it greatly in humility. It follows from this that the soul approaches God with greater reverence, convinced of its own nothingness.

It now knows God in a new way that gives it a higher, more exact concept of Him. The knowledge of its indigence and poverty also renders the soul more indulgent in its judgments of its neighbor, and its fraternal charity becomes more delicate. Particularly, the soul learns to do good works no longer for the enjoyment that it finds in them, as it did at first, which was the basis of many imperfections. It remains deprived of these sensible comforts and learns to act by pure will, and this is a big step for it in the spiritual life. Yes, with this trial the soul passes from the stage of sensibility, on which its exterior life habitually used to move, to the spiritual stage, in which, little by little, it is freed from the influence of sensible impressions, which render life unstable, like the impressions themselves. The soul becomes much more stable, even in its desire of perfection, because the fear that it experienced of no longer serving God has kindled within it a greater desire of being faithful and of never turning back. It is true, therefore, that this night of aridity and the nascent contemplation that is beginning in it, are for the soul what the saint calls "crusty bread," hard bread but made of pure wheat, which truly nourishes, while the milk of comforts and consolations was but child's food. To be sure, it was not useless, because the state of infancy also has its proper food, but obviously there is great progress when one can leave the milk aside and take more-solid food. This more-solid food is contemplation, which has begun to take the place of meditation. It is only a matter of the beginning of this great grace, or rather of the beginning of its first degree, but this is already precious for the soul and puts it on the way of contemplative union with God. So there is reason to give thanks to the Lord for this.

For that reason, the soul is not dismayed if it experiences aridity together with other, more-exterior trials. Since it is a matter of purification that tends to free the soul from all attachments that hinder its union with God, the soul should not be surprised if the Lord is not contented with detaching it just from what is of comfort to the spirit in the spiritual life. The spirit is not attached just to these consolations; most often, it is also attached to many external things: to goods of fortune, to health, to its good name, to the favor of others; or else it takes complacency in its natural gifts, of the control it believes it has over itself, of its interior peace, which it imagines is unalterable. Then we see that the Lord permits temptations of all kinds to come to it, uneasiness and scruples, anxiety and darkness that make it waver uncertainly on the way of virtue and force it to be guided like a little child to the great mortification of its self-love. Misfortunes deprive it of its property, or death robs it of its dear ones and its friends. Everything that to the eyes of the world can seem accidental, and that to the soul little experienced in the things of God could seem like punishments from the Lord, are instead so many divine mercies with which the Lord comes in contact with the soul to give it more freedom of spirit and thus prepare it for union with Him.

Naturally, in these circumstances, one cannot but suffer. When something to which we are attached is torn from us, it is impossible not to feel the wrench. But if the soul understands that the One who is testing it is its God, whom it is seeking with all its heart, and that precisely for that reason He is much more eagerly seeking to draw near to it, the soul — strengthened as it is by contemplative love — willingly accepts the trial and kisses the divine hand that administers death in order to give it life.

We shall see further on that, just at this time, the soul is invited to cultivate the spirit of faith, which makes it recognize the dispositions of divine providence in all events. Seeing in its suffering an invitation to greater perfection coming from the one whom it loves, the soul lovingly says its yes to Him.

Mysterious are the ways of the Lord. It would seem that aridity should deprive the soul of its spiritual treasure, and instead it enriches it immensely; it would seem that, in testing the soul, the Lord is giving vent to His wrath, and instead the temptations themselves are instruments of the divine mercy. How good the Lord is with the soul that loves Him! What a benefit for us to be able to understand it!

6

The Prayer of Faith

On leaving the night of aridity and its concomitant trials, do not believe that the work of the soul's sanctification is terminated, and that the soul is on the point of attaining union with God. We have seen only that the soul is withdrawn from creatures, to which its sensibility was too attached, and yet not sufficiently under control. Now we must consider how it comes close to God in a positive manner. Not that it has not already done so in some way, simply because it has learned to pray better, and every prayer is an elevation of our spirit to God; but this first period of the spiritual life has been above all a liberation of the soul from the bonds of disorderly affections, from the attachments and satisfactions for which one's sensibility is avid. These hindrances being finally eliminated, the craving for union with God is set free in the soul. To sustain the soul, so that it may arrive at the coveted end, the saint invites it to the intense practice of the theological virtues.

Nothing could be more opportune! The theological virtues, according to the teachings of theology, place our soul properly in relation with God, the author and goal of its supernatural life. Let us not forget it: the life of intimacy with God, our union with Him, is a divine gift to which our nature has no right, and to this gift it is not even "proportioned." To know God such as He is, as we will be able to one day in heaven, is a divine favor that surpasses all our needs and natural capacities. If God had not revealed it to us, we would never have known anything of our sublime destiny. God such as He is in Himself, and no longer only God our Creator, is an object that our natural intellect cannot attain with its own powers.

In heaven, in order to enter into immediate intellectual contact with this object, we will have need of the "light of glory"; but even on earth, to orient ourselves toward Him as toward our supreme end, we absolutely have need of the "light of faith." In this life, faith substitutes for the light of glory that will be given us in heaven. What we shall see then, we believe now through faith. The object of the beatific vision and the object of faith are one, but the way of knowing it is different; the first is clear, the second is obscure. In both cases, our intellect adheres to God considered in His proper essence; it attains the Trinity in Unity.

Since we have not only to know, but also finally to attain, an object so far superior to our nature that, with regard to it we have no right, we would be incapable of reaching it with our own powers unless God gave us hope in addition to faith. This virtue makes us expect from the divine goodness and mercy the help necessary to attain the heights to which God invites us. Hope makes us be sure that the Lord will assist us to reach eternal life. It orients our will, then, toward God, in the ardent desire of possessing Him, and makes it tend wholly toward Him.

The first two theological virtues thus prepare the way for the third, for charity, which makes us love God, with whom we are to live one day, and which makes us love Him above all with a love of benevolence — that is, as the Supreme Being who merits that His creature consume itself entirely for Him. The theological virtues, therefore, orient our spirits toward God; they make us put God at the center of all our human activity. Granted that they, like all the virtues, have been put at our disposition by God, we can make use of them when we wish. The saint, to teach us to bring our spirits close to God in the most efficacious manner, can do nothing better than invite us to the intense exercise of the theological virtues.

The "Signs" of Beginning Contemplation

The soul, having fallen, without its fault, into aridity and recognizing in itself the traditional three signs, follows the counsels of the Mystical Doctor; that is, it refrains from all force in meditating and applies itself only to remain in the company of its God, gazing at Him with simple affectionate regard. After some time, it attains great peace.

Prayer has become easy for it, although its manner has completely changed. No longer are there the beautiful discourses, the copious considerations that roused it even sensibly at first, such sweet affections that it expressed with ardent words; all that has vanished, but it is substituted with something better. Hardly does the soul begin to pray than it is wholly recollected and quickly makes contact with God. Not that this is a matter of profound thoughts regarding Him; rather, under this regard, it feels itself somewhat poor. It has only an indistinct and general concept of the Lord, but in a certain way, it is aware of being with Him. It keeps Him company and looks at Him.

This glance keeps it united to Him, but still more does the love that permeates this regard keep it united. Even though it has no precise concept of God, a profound sense of His grandeur is developed in it. He appears to it so different from all creatures that — it feels this in its heart — nothing can be compared to Him. He is so far above everything! For its heart, He is truly the "only one"; it feels it can give its love to no one else; He merits all the affection of the creature.

When the soul reaches such a form of prayer, it can be tranquil.

Union with God

It is not useless to deal with this question. Experience teaches that, when souls have come this far, they have great need of being reassured. It will seem to them that they are doing little; they habitually fear not doing "enough" and thus falling into idleness and losing time.

Here also, our saint will reassure the soul, going over once more the three signs with which we have been able to distinguish purifying aridity, which introduces the soul to contemplation, from culpable or simply natural aridity. As it is now a question of recognizing contemplation as being no longer in its period of painful formation, but rather in the time in which it begins to be established in the soul, the saint will adapt his signs, especially the third, to this new phase of contemplation.

The first sign is that incapacity to meditate with the aid of distinct concepts, of which we have spoken, and which from now on remains almost stable in the soul. Nevertheless, one should not think that one is no longer to make use of any good thought; sometimes such remembrances will still be able to give the start to prayer or sustain its progress. They can be used, for example, to take it up again after a few moments of involuntary distraction. But the soul can no longer enclose itself, as before, in these thoughts. When tempted to do so, it immediately feels empty and arid; it should no longer seek its devotion in these. It may happen that on one day or another, a certain facility for developing a thought that has struck it may return, but that does not last. The soul quickly falls back again into its usual incapacity. The former fount of devotion is exhausted, dried up; it is necessary to look elsewhere.

The second sign is that which excludes a culpable incapacity to occupy itself with God, caused by the soul's renewed affections for creatures, affections that attract it and attempt to captivate it, distracting it from the Lord. For that reason, the soul that does not feel disposed to occupy itself in divine things with the work of the intellect, because it is not receiving any nourishment, should not even have the desire to run after creatures. This does not exclude a certain coming and going of the imagination, which is an annoyance for the soul and is far from arousing its interest; it can only — and it ought to do so — despise all that can disturb it.

The third sign is the most important, the most characteristic, and permits a definitive judgment. We quote the testimony of the saint:

> The soul finds pleasure in being occupied only in loving attention to God, without particular considerations, with interior peace, quiet and repose, without exercising acts of its powers, that is, of its memory, intellect, and will, at least with discursive acts, namely, going from one to the other. There remains to it only the attention and the general loving knowledge, as we have said, without its having any particular knowledge whatever.

This is positive, while the two first signs are negative. The soul remains occupied with God. Remember that it was like this also during its crisis of aridity, when it was anxious, fearful of no longer serving God, and for that reason was all taken up with painful remembrance of Him. Evidently this painful remembrance of the Lord proceeds from a sincere desire of serving Him, and therefore, this also, being wholly permeated with love, keeps it in a contact of cognition and affection with God, notwithstanding that to the soul it might seem otherwise. This was the beginning of a loving knowledge as yet only beginning, which, following the counsels of St. John of the Cross, the soul little by little has acquired and in which it now finds so much pleasure and so much peace. During the painful crisis, the anxious remembrance of the Lord took the place of meditation, and, in a new and at first stranger way, carried the soul to God; now this new way of turning to the Lord is the loving, peaceful attention to Him. The soul does not, therefore, remain in idleness; quite otherwise! The saint's explanation will make us see quite clearly that the soul is occupied in God.

The Mystical Doctor makes an analysis of this loving attention to God, indicating the principles that operate in it, and we will see that these principles are really the theological virtues, aided by a hidden and delicate influence of the gifts of the Holy Spirit.

In the general loving attention of God, the saint recognizes, first of all, an eminent exercise of faith.

He has particularly insisted on the loftiness of the object of faith, which is the same object offered to us in the beatific vision, only now we do not *see* it but only *believe* it. Our intellect, resting on the divine testimony, adheres to it with certainty, although in obscurity. This object is none other than God considered in Himself, no longer simply as our Creator, as we can know Him by means of our natural reason through creatures, but God considered in His very nature, in His divinity, in the mystery of His intimate Trinitarian life, which cannot be known with the powers of human reason alone.

We cannot form a concept that adequately expresses the very essence of God. It is true that a theologian in his speculations, based on the analogy between God and creatures, can form a concept of God that expresses His eminent perfection in a "negative" manner. Such a concept is the result of a study, of a theological meditation. In its pious meditation, the soul might be able to rise to the knowledge of God with a similar process, but we have already observed that at this point of spiritual development, the soul is incapable of meditating. It is simply "aware" of the divine grandeur, of God's supereminence, which so outdistances Him from creatures. It is thus that faith presents Him to us. But the soul does not seek to form a precise concept of this high perfection of God; besides, it would not succeed in expressing what it understands. It is contented with gazing at the divine grandeur, attending simply to Him, content with that sovereign perfection, with that immense love, with that condescending mercy. It thus keeps itself in the presence of God, without making any further effort.

Nevertheless, it understands that such knowledge of God being "intellectually" or "conceptually" very "poor," precisely because the soul does not exactly try to form concepts, it could not remain there for long if it were not instructed by another participant. Here, the soul comes to be effectively instructed by love. The saint has noted that this general attention to God is *loving.*

When the soul is bound to God with love, it comes in some way to have a certain relish for Him, especially when it is a matter of passive love, of the love in which the soul was attracted to God. The soul then perceives in a certain manner that it is love for the one for whom it was created and who alone can satisfy its aspirations toward the infinite. In its affectionate communications with the divine object, it feels it is really where it belongs. "We were made for Thee, O Lord," wrote St. Augustine, "and our soul is restless until it rests in Thee."

Here, the soul reposes in God, and indeed, through this, it feels much at peace. At the same time, it acquires a knowledge of Him in some experiential way. It is not a knowledge that can give it new concepts, new ideas regarding God; we have already seen that with regard to concepts, the soul is rather poor; but it acquires a certain "sense of God." This sense originates in the will; it has its roots in love, but it will necessarily have some reflection also in the understanding and in this way will come to enrich the soul's general attention to God, rendering it more pleasing and causing the regard of faith, permeated with love, to be fixed on God and to remain more easily settled in Him.

Not only this—and here the teaching of the saint is particularly suggestive—but it is more likely that the action of the gifts of the

Holy Spirit will facilitate the gaze of loving faith on God. Listen to the Mystical Doctor:

> The more the soul remains purely and totally recollected in faith, so much the more does it possess the infused charity of God, and the greater the amount of charity it contains, so much the more does charity illumine it and communicate to it the gifts of the Holy Spirit, because charity is the cause and the means through which it communicates them. (*Ascent* II, XXIX, 6)

We know that the property of the gifts of the Holy Spirit, especially of wisdom, to which the saint more frequently alludes, is to render our knowledge of God more savory. This latter is made therefore more pleasant and for that reason also more experiential. In this way, there is developed in the soul what we call the "sense of God," which is a new manner of knowing the Lord, and quite different from the purely conceptual and intellectual knowledge that can be had of Him.

This suffices for us to understand clearly that the general loving knowledge of God to which the soul attains after the crisis of aridity, and in which it now finds much pleasure, is not an inactive one in the sense that the soul no longer does anything. It supposes instead the use of our highest powers, the intellect and the will, now raised to the supernatural level by the light of faith, by the love of charity, and by the influence of the gifts of the Holy Spirit. For that reason, it is not a question of idleness, but solely of a simplification of their operations, which, from being discursive and leaning much on the imagination and the sensibility, have become more spiritual, more tranquil, and also more precious.

The soul that God has led by such a form of prayer does not believe that it is losing its time. It will experience by itself, however, that in this prayer its desire of "belonging to God" will become ever stronger. Still not having formulated particular resolutions at this time, it always leaves prayer more determined to give its whole self to the service of its God. Is not this enough to judge the fruitfulness of its prayer?

Contemplation Is to Be Preferred to Visions

St. John of the Cross teaches that this prayer is so fruitful and so precious that the soul not only ought not to regret the beautiful meditations of the past, but it ought to value this prayer much more than all the extraordinary favors that are sometimes granted to pious souls.

The saint puts us much on our guard against "visions and revelations" and points out that, most times, the enemy of our souls causes such phenomena in order to divert the soul from the intense practice of loving faith that it finds in the budding contemplation. The saint insists that it is not these favors, given their "particular" nature, that unite the soul to God; this office is reserved to the theological virtues, which, as we have seen, have for their object God Himself. Hence, the saint gives to the contemplative soul this most precious counsel. We have to admire its logical conformity with his doctrine on the supreme value of the theological virtues in the fulfillment of (the soul's) union with God. If, in prayer, some apparition of saints is presented to the soul, or if the soul is made to hear some words that seem supernatural, it is not to stop there but simply to take from it the hint to recollect itself again in God with a movement of loving faith. This will aid its continued ascent toward God much more efficaciously than all particular visions or revelations.

How far this is from the practice of too many imprudent souls, or from directors not less blameworthy who attribute an exaggerated importance to these insecure phenomena, and who sometimes base on them the whole direction of the souls that are experiencing them!

It should never be forgotten that, in all things of this sort, not only can the devil enter in, but even more the natural self, one's own fantasy, which, especially in temperaments that are a bit unbalanced or morbid (and it is not always easy to recognize them quickly), creates beautiful words and apparitions even of religious character. Yes, there can also be good apparitions that stir up devotion; the error begins when it is believed that they proceed directly from God and that one must take them into consideration for one's direction of life. Some souls, often ingenuous ones, feel themselves easily persuaded of this, so if they believe themselves favored by Him, they tell their spiritual director with full conviction: "Jesus thus said to me. The Lord wants this of me."

Fortunate are such souls when they meet a director who knows the doctrine of St. John of the Cross! He will try first to dissipate their preoccupations, teaching them to consider such things of no importance. If the soul does not succeed in this, the first rule the director will give it is "Pay no attention and make nothing of all that comes to your mind in this way, without having first referred it to me and having asked my advice." Even if he believes that it is the good spirit guiding the soul, judging it according to the traditional rules for the discernment of spirits, never will he permit it to do something suggested by a revelation if, taking into account the principles of faith, his reason does not show him the opportuneness of the thing suggested, without paying attention to that particular revelation.

If it were always done like this, many imprudences would be avoided, as well as much loss of time. I confess that, when I saw now and again the voluminous notebooks filled by similar visionaries, I said to myself many times: "Had they employed their time really praying and in serving their neighbor, it would have been more fruitful for them and for others, and less wearying for the director who was condemned to examine all their rubbish."

Whatever be the origin — even supernatural — of these manifestations, in our life of union with God, they ought always to give way to the exercise of the theological virtues, to contemplation in which the glance of loving faith introduces us to an intimacy with God destined to increase and to be established in the soul.

St. Teresa of Jesus has wonderfully described in her writings the forms that contemplation can assume, which, taking a more distinctly passive character, communicates to the soul a sense of the divine presence. Sometimes the soul is recollected so profoundly that it loses all possibility of being distracted; other times, the imagination continues to weary it. That happens precisely from the fact that, having arrived at this point, the soul knows God more through love than through the intellect, which now does not form entirely distinct concepts and so does not make use of the imagination at all. The latter remains free and left to itself, and therefore easily happens to annoy the soul, when it is not absorbed in a more abundant divine sweetness that, enjoyed by the will, superabounds with even more force in the intellect and absorbs it in God.

It happens sometimes that the divine communication is so vehement as not to be supported by the soul; then the person falls into an "ecstasy." In reference to this, let us note immediately that the Mystical Doctor, far from exaggerating the importance of the ecstatic phenomenon, in which some ancient and modern psychologists have believed the foundation of the mystical life consists, considered it instead as a weakness, from which the soul is freed when it goes through the dark night of the spirit, which is to dispose it immediately for union with God.

Every soul that happens to be rewarded by God with contemplation does not, for this reason, necessarily experience all the forms, nor are all of them necessary to lead the soul to deep union with

God. In this field, the Lord makes the choice, and the soul should be content with the path that He traces out for it. Whatever be the form of contemplation to which the Lord calls it, high or lowly, vehement or sweet, manifest or hidden, this contemplation always remains an intense exercise of the theological virtues aided by the gifts of the Holy Spirit. It raises the soul above all visions and particular revelations, its extraordinary phenomena and ecstasies, and makes of it an efficacious instrument for union with God. We shall see a little further on that, in the same state of union, contemplation maintains the soul almost continuously in contact with God.

The Spirit of Faith

Having reached contemplation, the soul then lives intensely a life of faith, especially during the time of prayer; but it does not cultivate the virtue less in the midst of its daily occupations. It learns to view all it meets in life in this supernatural light, which shows it all events, great and small, in relation to divine providence.

Faith, like the beatific vision, is a participation in divine knowledge given to us. As God necessarily knows creatures in relation to Himself, so also faith presents them subordinate to Him; this is, however, a much more comprehensive and realistic view of the world than just a view of creatures on their own — that is, of secondary causes without reference to the First Cause. Many Christians have too abstract a concept of divine providence.

They know that it governs the universe, but they do not figure in concrete terms the real significance of this truth. They do not understand that nothing, absolutely nothing, happens in the world, not even free human actions, that is not under divine control.

Not that God has submitted everything to the law of necessity, or that He positively wills all that free creatures do. No, many of our actions — all our sinful actions, for example — He does not will, but He simply tolerates them, not hindering what is done, precisely because He respects the liberty of creatures to whom, in His wisdom, He has given this great prerogative, yet foreseeing that many will abuse it. Allowing that rebellious creatures regret their actions, He makes these latter re-enter the divine plan with which He achieves His highest ends, particularly the salvation and sanctification of souls. There is no human action that can escape from this divine control with which He disposes all things for the good of those whom He loves: "All things work together to the good of those who love God" (see Rom. 8:28).

The soul of faith, for whom divine providence is a concrete fact, sees that in all events, God comes to meet it with His divine invitations to greater perfection.

"Everything that happens," said a chosen soul, "is for me a message of the excessive love of God for my soul" (Blessed Elizabeth of the Trinity).

These souls, in all events, see not only the action of creatures — that is, of the second cause; for example, of that person who annoys them or this other who, in the aversion shown, seeks to harm them. Over and above these, they see their God, who, allowing creatures to act imperfectly, gives occasion for the practice of an act of virtue, perhaps heroic, and positively invites them to accomplish it. A soul of faith lives more with God than with creatures, more with the First Cause than with second causes. Do not forget that these latter are also real and need to be taken into account, but for the soul, the first reality is God, and "first of all" applies always to Him. Is not God the Father of our human family? Is it not just, then, that, although wishing to give the children their place, we nevertheless give the first place to the Father, to whom it truly belongs? The soul of faith knows the divine transcendence and supereminence so well that it gives this first place to God totally and spontaneously.

Union with God

Besides, the soul of faith can recognize its Lord wherever He is. That very own God, whose grandeur it enjoys in contemplation, it adores present in its soul, in which He has fixed His dwelling. It acknowledges Him in the person of Jesus Christ, the divine Savior whose human life it studies. The same faith contemplates this God made man in the tabernacles of our churches, where He resides and awaits our visits and our homage. Moreover, faith tells the soul that God makes His will known to it in the orders of its superiors, especially ecclesiastical, and that Jesus, the Incarnate Word, wishes to be served in His brethren. He has said that He will consider as done to Him all that we do to those who are His, for the souls redeemed by His Blood.

The soul of faith, therefore, meets its God everywhere and everywhere sees Him as the one who invites it to be good, generous, and holy. With the dispositions of His divine providence, He gives it occasions to become so.

Oh, if in our life we would truly give to God the place He deserves, the place that faith makes us see is truly His, how transformed our life would be! Let us accept adversity with much greater resignation, knowing that it does not come to us without the knowledge of our heavenly Father, who, while not approving the evil action of the person who causes us anguish, is powerful enough to make the untoward event become a part of the plan of love with which He accomplishes our good. Certainly, God did not will the terrible trial of the war that we have gone through. He, by means of His vicar on earth—who truly did everything possible to avert it—cried with a strong voice to the nations to abstain from it. But men wanted it; and it came with all its disastrous consequences, from which we are suffering and who knows how much we shall still have to suffer.

Who could reasonably claim that God ought to prevent the consequences of human actions that He did not will? His mercy, however, moves Him to pardon His creature when it humbly asks pardon and to come to its aid. The rebellious creature does not know enough even to do this and remains obstinate in its pride. God nevertheless, in His omnipotent knowledge, draws good even from evil; from trials caused by the wicked, He draws good for good souls. For many, the tribulations of the war have been occasions of new spiritual ascents. Many times, I have had occasion to verify this and to admire the divine delicacy with which He comes to meet generous souls, to render them heroic and thus prepare them for union with Him.

Faith lived with intensity draws the soul powerfully to God. In contemplation, it puts the intellect in contact with the divine supereminence, while the love and activity of the gifts of the Holy Spirit render its knowledge loving and pleasant, giving the soul a precious sense of God that induces it to want to give Him all the room He merits.

Faith shows our souls the place that God truly occupies in the universe and in the daily events in which our souls move. Our faith shows us that we move continuously by divine dispositions, all of which intend to procure in the best way our salvation and sanctification. It is most valuable for our souls to know and acknowledge this. It is more valuable still to be able to arrange our whole lives in dependence on the principles of faith.

We will be aided in this by hope and charity.

7

Hope and Pure Love

Faith makes us advance greatly in our ascent toward God because, with the knowledge of Him that it procures for us, it puts Him before us as the end to which we must tend. It makes us encounter Him in everything; it makes us live in the midst of everything by the paternal dispositions with which He continually invites us to ascend. Further along it brings us hope, which makes us rest our whole lives upon Him. Charity will then come to create the bond that will bind our will so strongly to God's as to transform our wills into His, thus bringing about that which is most fundamental in the state of union.

Having studied the exercise of faith by the light of the teachings of St. John of the Cross, we must also learn from him to live charity and love more intensely. We will concentrate mostly on the Lord, and our intimacy with Him will grow by practice.

Hope: Its Nature

It seems that many Christians in our time have lost what might be called the "sense of eternal life." They believe, it is true, but, practically, in their ordinary lives, they make little account of it. They seem solely intent on acquiring the goods of this world; these, in fact, occupy their minds, rouse their preoccupations, and are the aim of their efforts.

I do not mean by this to say that Christians who live in the world must be disinterested regarding earthly goods that they need for assuring either their own lives or those of their families. A certain solicitude for acquiring earthly goods can even be praiseworthy; but it is a matter of keeping everything in its place and, above all, of giving God His place.

Once a human has been ordered by God to the attainment of eternal union with Him, do you perhaps find it reasonable that we make so little of it? It is not a trifling matter to know that we, for all eternity, shall be able to enjoy intimacy with the divine Persons, who will admit us into society with them, and to know that the degree of this intimacy will depend on the degree of love that we have acquired on earth with the supernatural practice of the virtues. Either we believe it, or we do not believe it. If we believe it, then why not make it effectively the sublime goal of our life? If we truly seek this supreme good above all things, we will more easily succeed in putting all other goods in their place, by not attaching our hearts to them, by not letting them absorb us.

Not even the spontaneous solicitude that we have for the welfare of our dear ones should succeed in troubling our mind and heart with anxious preoccupation about acquired news. Even regarding our loved ones, our first desire should be to procure their eternal good. We will thus give more importance to their spiritual welfare, which will assure it, than to their material welfare, which so many times is the sole preoccupation of certain people who would like to call themselves Christians, but in reality are not—or are hardly such.

While we urge the desire for the possession of God, we must refute a certain objection: it is said sometimes—almost in memory of the famous and not-too-pleasant dispute between Jacques-Bénigne Bossuet and François Fénelon about "pure love"—that it is not opportune to concentrate the soul's regard on reward, be it even heavenly, because that would come to create in us a "mercenary" spirit, and shut the soul up in itself in the search for its own good instead of God's. The soul needs, instead, to love God with the highest disinterestedness. As if opposition could exist between the theological virtues, and hope could be opposed to love!

St. John of the Cross has never taken up antinomies of this kind. He also had a doctrine of pure love, and we will expound it further on, but it does not, in fact, exclude the love of hope. On the contrary, the love of hope, well cultivated and concentrating all our desires on God, greatly facilitates the continual practice of love, which would be much more difficult to achieve if the hope of attaining union with Him did not divert our preoccupation from created objects. We must not forget, however, that the same heavenly joy in us may proceed from our actions with which we glorify God in a most excellent manner.

We intelligent creatures are created to glorify the Lord with acts of intellect and will—that is, with acts of knowledge and love—and in life eternal, we will know and love the Lord in the most perfect manner. Consequently, eternal life does not shut us up in ourselves, but it orients us even more toward God and makes us attend to His glory more than ever. The Mystical Doctor, in his *Spiritual Canticle*, has admirably taught that we are going to heaven to love God, and therefore, the whole of heavenly life does not consist only in receiving, but also in giving. If it is true that, with the beatific vision, the blessed soul receives God, then, with the love that necessarily springs from it, the blessed soul gives itself irrevocably to the Lord, adhering to Him with all its powers. Just so, the blessed soul will eternally glorify the Lord in the same measure of its blessedness. The more the soul possesses the Lord, so much the more will it love Him.

How is it possible that a soul that, during its whole earthly life, learned to find its glory in giving itself generously to the Lord can be happy in heaven if there, too, it cannot give itself to the Lord? Great souls, especially those formed in the school of the Mystical Doctor, as was St. Thérèse of the Child Jesus, have always understood how. In her doctrine of love, the saint of Lisieux leaned directly on our master, whose *Spiritual Canticle* and *Living Flame* she had deeply appreciated. Even in the last days of her life, she loved to nourish her soul with notes taken from these marvelous works. When a Sister was speaking of the joy that she would taste in Paradise in the company of the saints, she replied: "It is not that which makes my heart beat: it is the love that I will receive and that I will be able to give!"

The little saint even wanted to go to heaven in order to love. It is therefore absurd to want to represent heavenly beatitude as a species of egotistical pleasure, thus preferring the cold attitude of the philosopher who, like Kant, wishes to act solely "through duty," in the austere satisfaction of being able to say: "I have done my duty," as if man then might not once again shut himself up in himself. Does it not appear nobler and less egotistical to do one's duty in order to succeed in loving God eternally in heaven, than to do it to procure for one's personality the perfection of moral rectitude? St. John of the Cross thought so.

The Need to Cultivate Hope

Yes, in our lives, we need to make ample room for the desire for God. We need to cultivate this aspiration and to nurture in our hearts the solicitude for the things necessary to attain the possession of God. We also need to nourish a great trust in Him who, in His goodness and mercy, wants to help us realize our hope. In short: we need to cultivate hope either for its purpose or for its motive.

To cultivate it in its purpose brings to mind the formula of the act of hope I learned as a little child, which stated so well the true great objects of this virtue. We were taught to say what we await with confidence from the Lord and through the merits of Jesus Christ: the pardon of our sins, the grace to live good lives, and, in the end, eternal life. Yes, as the last good, eternal life, but then also all that is necessary to get there and, therefore, first of all, pardon for my sins. How comforting it is to know that the Lord asks me to be certain of His pardon, every time that I am truly sorry for my sins and show the reality of my repentance by wanting to confess them, as He has ordained.

Sin is an obstacle to a holy life; I must therefore have faith that, if I am sorry, the Lord will remove the obstacle to my holiness. That is not all; after the negative side, there is the positive side. The Lord will take away the obstacle and positively also give me help, "the grace to live a good life," to live according to my condition, according to my vocation, but a truly good life, morally good and therefore holy. The Lord wants me to trust in His help so that I may become holy.

Oh yes, the Lord wants me to be certain of this! It is not a matter of intellectual certainty, but of a certainty of heart—namely, of that extreme confidence that makes one say to someone: "I put my trust in you." Theology teaches that such trust is the very characteristic of perfect hope. The Lord wants us to tend to the perfection of the virtues, and for that reason He desires that we put our trust in Him.

It is easy to see that in cultivating this sense of certainty about the divine aid, in order to attain the highest good, we must become, in some way, strong with the very strength of God, who, we know, wants to help us. When it is a question of possessing Him, the trust of a soul of goodwill can be sublime. St. John of the Cross has given us in this regard the maxim that St. Thérèse of the Child Jesus loved to repeat: "We obtain from God as much as we hope from Him" (*The Dark Night* II, XXI, 8). Note that the maxim was written by the saint with reference to the soul that has concentrated all the desires of its life on the attainment of eternal union with God.

Union with God

This truly is hoping: to make of eternal life our supreme aim that dominates and subordinates to itself all our other desires. Such will spontaneously be the attitude of a soul that lives as a true child of God. Our paternal home is heaven. There we must arrive, and there we shall truly feel in our place.

Let us seek, therefore, to live well, and let us also hope confidently from God the grace to live well, and after that—why not?—the grace to attain while still on earth that state of union that is a pledge of the heavenly union. We must become saints: this is the will of God, and He wants us to feel certain of His help to attain the goal.

How much more courageous does the soul feel, and how easily does it become more generous, when it thus nurtures its hope in the Lord! This hope will become a loving confidence in the heavenly Father and, in its turn, will develop into the most absolute abandonment, since the soul, sure that God wishes to sanctify it and knowing through its spirit of faith that He governs all the events of the world, leaves the sanctifying to Him.

"He will know how to dispose everything in a better way for carrying out my and His desire," thinks this soul. "Let Him choose the way; He sees more clearly and farther than I. I place my trust entirely in Him!"

Then, according to what St. Thérèse of the Child Jesus taught, the soul becomes like a babe in the arms of his mother and "in the midst of the agitations of the world, sleeps tranquilly in the arms of the Lord." It always remains serene in possession of itself; for that reason, it is capable of employing all its strength in the service of the Lord without wasting it in useless agitations.

Purification of the Memory

According to the teachings of the saint, the purification of the memory proceeds from the exercise of faith. Faith has made us give first place in our intellect to the thought of God, the First Cause, which is superior to second causes. In the life of prayer, faith has also made us give first place to loving and contemplative attention to God, above all to meditative thoughts, precious though they may be, yet less precious than this "sense of God" that gives birth to contemplative prayer. Obviously, faith brings the intellect close to God. In an analogous way, hope concentrates our memory on Him.

We know by experience that the memory dwells more frequently on the recollections of things that we love and of those that we fear: of those that we love, because in them are determined the various aims and purposes of our lives, which are so many motives for arousing our industrious impulses; of those that we fear, because we see them as so many forces that can hinder us from attaining our goals. These are the sources of our agitations and of the infinite solicitudes that do not give peace to our spirit and keep us preoccupied, troubled, and at times render us quite unhappy.

In a soul that cultivates an intense desire for eternal life and in which this desire effectively dominates every other solicitude, the objects of its aspirations are loved with great moderation, with much more reserve—that is, with greater conformity and abandonment to the divine will. In the memory, the thought of those aspirations is less stirred up; and, on the other hand, the soul certain of its God, believing with lively faith that the loving, divine providence disposes all things for its eternal good, fears adverse forces much less, as it knows well that those forces cannot break loose if God does not permit it. Even in such a case, their action will necessarily enter into the plan of divine providence. The soul that cultivates supernatural hope succeeds in remaining serene in the midst of the most painful tribulations. It does not fall into the idleness of quietism, because it knows that it is the will of the Lord that in our needs we also put our hand to the work. Once it has generously done its duty, it entrusts itself as a child to its heavenly

Father, saying: "You take care of it, Lord; I will think of You!" and abandons itself courageously to His providential dispositions, certain that its own good and that of so many other souls must result from the divine plan.

Thus, hope also, in its own way, makes the soul live with God, makes it tend to the possession of Him and to having recourse continually to His aid so as to reach the most beautiful and legitimate desires.

Charity

If faith and hope bring us close to God, the love of charity unites us to Him.

In his works, St. John of the Cross, true doctor of divine love, has, in a marvelous manner, treated of love in all its aspects. Nevertheless, we must say that his treatment of passive love is more complete than that of active love, with which we now intend to concern ourselves. Later on, we will deal more extensively with passive love, when we shall be treating of the supreme trials of the soul or of the state of contemplative union, to which the soul attains through these trials. The saint has left us an exhaustive study of them in the second book of *The Dark Night* and in a large part of *The Spiritual Canticle* and of *The Living Flame of Love*. In the third book of *The Ascent of Mount Carmel*, he had intended to treat abundantly of active love, with which the soul starts out toward union by means of its own application. He had expounded at length on the conduct that the soul should adopt regarding the goods that life presents to it, if it does not wish to be attached to them and thus hinder its union with God but wishes instead to make use of them for His greater glory.

In his exposition, he developed a method of conduct for the soul with regard to spiritual goods themselves, which naturally has a more intimate relation to progress in the interior life; but at this point the saint's treatment of the subject was left unfinished.

He had differentiated the diverse spiritual goods in various classes, the first of which was that of perfecting spiritual goods. These would certainly have been most interesting, because the very word "perfecting" seems to indicate that which would directly contribute to render love perfect, but the saint never got around to writing this part.

Nevertheless, from the whole of his doctrine and from the spiritual documentation that can be gathered from various writings and from letters, it is not too difficult to establish what for him were the sources from which should spring the perfection of love. They are obviously the purity and strength of love itself.

Pure Love

In various places in his writings, the saint speaks of "pure love," but with him this expression has nothing to do, at least directly, with the concept discussed in the famous controversy between Bossuet and Fénelon to which we have alluded. In substance, that controversy was a question of deciding whether a soul fully aware of the love of God can, in the supernatural life, leave out of consideration the love of hope — that is, to arrive at a state in which it will never more have recourse to the lever of heavenly recompense to move it to good, but will act always for God and reject every demand for its own happiness. Such a problem seems never to have occurred to the saint's mind; on the contrary, he invites the soul to nourish itself equally on hope and on charity. Certainly, he never saw in the increase of hope an obstacle to charity, which, for him, reaches its highest perfection when the soul is united with God in eternal beatitude. Indeed, then it begins to love God indefectibly with all its strength. The love of hope thus remains ordered to the love of pure charity as to its end. For our saint, pure love is uniquely the love that in its exercise has become pure and simple benevolence. So it is that the soul, loving God, does not seek its own satisfaction, but solely that of its Beloved.

We humans are much inclined to pleasure, and we spontaneously seek satisfaction in the noblest of our actions, spoiling in that way the purity of our intention.

We do the same thing many times also in the love of God. In love, we easily experience pleasure, and if, in the love of God, this enjoyment of ours should form our motive, in the very same love of God we are seeking ourselves. Therefore, it is evident that our activity of love, in the measure in which it seeks its personal satisfaction, is not directed to God, but ends instead in us. The result is that a part of our love and the strength and energy that we put into it is lost from the supernatural point of view. For that reason, it is of the highest importance for the soul that it learn to love God "purely"—that is to say, seeking in its love nothing but His pleasure and in no way to find its own satisfaction.

To educate our souls well in pure love, the saint has taught us to distinguish the sentiment and the operation in love, showing the very relative value of the first and the substantial quality of the second.

In all of us, love—even the love of God—is easily accompanied by sentiment. First of all, because of love, we have two faculties: the will and the heart, the seat of our sensibility. It suffices to reflect a moment to understand that the noblest, highest, most spiritual, and therefore most truly "human" of these two faculties is the will. We really refer to the act of the will when we say that to love means to wish a person well. The expression that we spontaneously use (in Italian) to attest our love is "I wish you well."[7] It is true that

---

[7] In English we simply say, "I love you." —Trans.

when our will loves, the heart is also easily, although not always, united with it. Love is pleasant to the heart in a special way; it takes delight in feeling itself seized by a strong and impassioned love. A soul that loves God can feel its love also in the heart and can love its God with ardent transport. In this case, in the love of God, the soul also experiences pleasure and satisfaction.

It is not only the heart that is capable of sentiment. The will can feel itself strongly inclined toward the person loved; it, too, takes pleasure in feeling itself strongly drawn toward its beloved. The soul that feels its will seized to such a degree by the Lord as to be prompt in detaching itself still more, just to please Him, experiences at the same time a great joy, which renders the burden of sacrifice light.

All that is quite all right, and one should not think that the Lord does not value our love when it is accompanied by sentiment. In His first commandment, He enjoined us to love Him also "with our whole heart"—that is, with all our capacity to love, consequently also with the sensible capacity of the heart. But because in love, accompanied by sentiment, there is danger that our nature, avid for satisfaction, may also be satisfying itself, it is necessary that a soul desirous of using its whole capacity and all its strength for the Lord alone, and not losing even a crumb in looking for something outside of Him, be careful not to allow the purity of its love to be diminished by tolerating as motive the seeking of its own pleasure.

For this reason, the saint explains the immense difference between the spiritual value of the act of love and the value of the sentiment. The operation of love is the act of the will with which we love God; and what is the good that we rational and free creatures can desire from our God if not "that His will be done in us, with full active and passive adhesion"? With this adhesion, a spiritual creature, gifted with intelligence and will, procures in the best way the glory of its Creator, since, indeed, we have been created for "the honor and glory of God." To love God, then, means practically to adhere in such a complete way to the will of God as to lose our will in His.

The saint manifests the supreme spiritual value of this operation of the soul, saying: "With the operation of love the soul is united to God." This is clear, although the state of union, as we have stated above, consists in having lost our will in that of God.

The condition of sentiment is completely different. The saint affirms clearly "that it does not unite (the soul) to God" but is only a pleasant impression of our ego. In fact, it is only an accompaniment of love, which does not in any way belong to its substance and of which the soul, therefore, has no need in order to love truly. On the contrary, as we have seen, its presence is often for the soul an occasion to fall back a little on itself, even in the exercise of divine love, and that manifestly constitutes an imperfection.

If it is an imperfection, it is necessary that the soul that desires to reach the fullness of divine love free itself from it. For that reason, the saint instructs us to make little account of sentiment in love and to attach ourselves solely to loving God, cost what it may.

In reality, the soul can do much with its own application, but it must be convinced that by itself, it will never be able to reach the end, total purity of love, and so the Lord comes to meet it. In the crisis of aridity of which we have spoken, the Lord has begun His work, freeing the soul from sensible attachments and teaching it thus to make little of those sweet emotions of love that pleased it so much when it used to make its tasty meditations. By means of aridity the Lord led it to the love of the will.

Since even in the will there is a peaceful sentiment to which the will could attach itself, we shall see that the Lord will come to free it from this also, with an interior trial more painful than aridity, but in which love, immersed in the crucible, will come out completely purified. This will be the most painful and dark "night of the spirit," of which we shall treat further on. The teachings on pure love—that is, on the love for which the soul spends all its strength for the Lord, to love without falling back on itself—are therefore fundamental in the thought of the saint and give the key to a profound exposition (of the trial), be it of aridity or of spiritual desolations, that each soul that wants to attain union with God normally has to go through.

Strong Love

We were saying that the saint also wrote about "strong" love. When he began his treatise on love, in the third book of *The Ascent*, he insisted especially on the Lord's precept of loving Him "with all our strength," wishing to indicate that love should come to the point of taking in hand all the levers of control of our human nature—that is, governing all our faculties and applying them to actions for the sole end of the glory of God, to whom pure love uniquely tends. But—as we said—his work was interrupted, and the saint did not finish explaining, as he intended, this influx of love on all our operations and how the soul, in a practical way, is to reach this point.

It seems evident that, to attain such a dominion of love, an intense love is required, one that is rooted so deeply in the soul that it rings spontaneously and continuously from its depths and gives impulse to all its actions. For this reason, to know in what way strong love—a love, namely, that dominates the whole life of the soul—is attained, it suffices to know practically in what way the intensity of love increases in the soul in the most efficacious manner.

On this point, the saint's disciples have given us the clearest theoretical and practical teachings. We find the theoretical teachings in the noted theological work of the Discalced Carmelites of

Salamanca.[8] The practical teachings come to us from a saint very
dear to us, St. Thérèse of the Child Jesus, who, in her whole doctrine,
depends on our master. The Salamanca theologians teach us that
the increase of the intensity of charity in us depends to the greatest
extent on our virtuous actions—that is, on our good works done
under the influence of charity. Every work accomplished merits an
increase of charity. But that merited increase is not always granted
immediately; it is often given with part in reserve and will be granted
to the soul only when it enters heaven. In this case, the merit we
acquire can be compared to the interest that, while produced by
the capital, is not accumulated with it, but remains apart, yet being owned by the one who acquired it, and thus the capital is not
increased. When, instead, the interest comes together with the
capital, the latter is augmented; the following year it produces more
fruit, and so on. At times, the increase of love caused by meritorious
works is also quickly joined with our capital of love, and so makes it
increase, immediately augmenting in this way the intensity of our
love. This is verified every time we perform our good actions with
all the love of which we are capable—that is, when we perform
them not against our will but with all our heart. Then it is as if our
heart opens to receive the increase of love that we merit and that
unites with the love already existing, thus adding to its intensity.

Each one may thus see the great importance—for anyone who
desires to reach perfect love—of striving to do all one's works well
"with all one's heart," overcoming one's inertia and natural pettiness.

As a matter of fact, this is the reason certain souls, while still
good, seem always stationary, while others, whenever they are met
with in course of time, have always progressed in fervor. The reason
is that the former perform their good works with some negligence,

---

[8] Salmaticenses, *Cursus theologicus*, *Tr. De Charitate. De augmento
charitatis.*

without wanting to weary themselves too much, while the others are generous and end up recompensed with a continual increase of love.

Indeed, this practice was recommended by St. Thérèse of the Child Jesus: "Do everything for love, singing, with a smile on your lips," to show the Lord that we do it gladly, with all our heart.

"I will sing, yes, I will always sing," wrote the little saint, "even if I have to gather my roses amid thorns" (*Story of a Soul* XI).

To her works of charity and her works of penance she endeavored to add that "smile" so characteristic of her soul that revealed her immense love and her glorious serenity. She is the "saint of the smile."

And the fruit of this practice? An immense love!

"Lord," wrote Saint Thérèse shortly before her death, "Your love has gone before me from my infancy; it has grown with me, and now it is an abyss whose depths I cannot fathom" (*Story of a Soul* X). And with this unfathomable love she loved her Lord and directed to Him alone all her actions and all her suffering. In her love, she became truly strong and "fulfilled." And this was not a privilege of the saint; it was simply the fulfillment of the law of love's increase: when we do everything wholeheartedly, love grows continually.

Splendid are St. John of the Cross's teachings on hope and charity. The soul that practices them with diligence "runs" along the spiritual ways and advances more each day in divine intimacy. It looks at the reality of life with the faith that sees everything in relation to God. It trusts completely in the strength of God with a lively hope and attaches itself to Him with a love whose intensity, force, and purity increase continually. Such a soul finds itself on the road to union and lives already in company with God. Much more than before does it seek God, and consequently more than in the past will "its lover, the Lord, seek the soul." Of this jealous divine search we shall now treat.

8

Jesus Our Guide

St. Thérèse of the Child Jesus, who was one day to reach the summit of the mountain of love, where union of the soul with God is perfected, in one of those periods of aridity, trial, and darkness that are inevitable in the spiritual ascents, thus described the state of her soul:

> Our Lord took me by the hand and made me enter a subterranean tunnel, where it was neither cold nor hot, where there was no sunlight, and not even the rain nor the wind found access; an underground passage where I saw nothing but a semi-veiled glimmer shed on the interior from the lowered eyes of the face of Jesus.... I did not see any progress toward the end of our journey, because it was made underground; nevertheless it seemed to me that without knowing how, we were nearing the summit of the mountain. (Letter IV to M. Agnes)

In the midst of this darkness Thérèse was tranquil and in peace, sure of reaching the end, because her guide, barely seen, held her by the hand. This guide was Jesus.

Before undertaking the study in St. John of the Cross of the darkest, most painful part of the way that leads to divine union, where the soul passes through the trial called by the saint the "passive night of the spirit," we also want to remind the soul that it does not have to face this suffering alone. The Mystical Doctor shows it the guide, the companion, the spouse, who will take it lovingly by the hand and make its steps safe: Jesus Christ, the Incarnate Word, true man and true God; Jesus our way and our end, Jesus our all. We want to take this occasion to explain in a substantially complete way what may be, in its various aspects, the attitude that, according to St. John of the Cross, the contemplative soul desirous of union with God ought to have, in its whole spiritual life, toward Jesus Christ, the Son of God and the second Person of the Most Holy Trinity, made man to work out our salvation and sanctification.

For St. John of the Cross, Jesus is not only the master and model of the soul, who ought to listen to His teachings and conform to His example; He is also its spouse, who, giving it a share in His own life, works in it, by means of grace, that which He teaches it by means of doctrine. Jesus is also the object of the soul's contemplation, which lovingly receives nourishment from the mystery of the redeeming Incarnation.

Jesus, Master and Model

In truth, it is not enough to say that St. John of the Cross proposes Christ to us as master and model. It should be said that he presents Him as "beloved" master and as "loved" model, to whom, since we love Him, we wish to conform ourselves; and, as He has conquered our heart, we wish to embrace His teachings.

I begin by recalling that the first preoccupation of the saint is to install Jesus in our hearts. He has recourse to the lever of the love of Jesus, to move the soul to enter with energy on the way of abnegation, which should lead it progressively to union with God.

Having studied the doctrine of the saint, we are in a position to embrace with a single glance the whole journey we must travel to reach the goal. We have learned that the first task consists principally in becoming masters of the sensibility that urges us too strongly toward earthly satisfactions. The soul prepares to work with the firm decision to control the use of its senses and to discipline its passions. The exercises proposed by the saint require energy, but the soul, agreeing to them, has proved itself to be truly seeking the Lord. He (the Lord) has also come to seek it and does so with the crisis of aridity, by means of which the soul has succeeded in rendering its interior life less dependent on sensibility, and therefore it becomes more solidly spiritual.

Thus placed in the "way of the spirit," the soul has tried to draw near to the Lord by means of an intense exercise of the theological virtues, which truly introduced it to a continual and rather intimate relationship with God. Its "active" search for the Lord was in this way intensified; therefore, it is to be expected that the Lord also will come again to look for it.

We are now coming to the study of the crises that are to bring to an end the purification of the spirit to prepare the soul immediately for union. The way of union has two preparation periods: the purification of the senses and the purification of the spirit; and in both there is an active and a passive phase. In order that the soul may courageously undertake the first phase of its way, the saint appeals to the soul's love for Jesus. Then, to avoid its retreating in fear before the suffering of the second—namely, of the purification of the spirit—he will remind it of the annihilation that its beloved Jesus reached.

Let us remember that, from the first steps on the way of union, the saint proposed to the soul a program of energetic renunciation, precisely so that it would not lose time in useless wanderings and could thus soon reach the end. It is a matter of a continual war against our natural inclinations, and we recall again the strained and almost painful impression that, in the beginning, the saint's sentences made on us: "Not to that which is easiest, but to that which is most difficult; not to the most pleasant, but to the least pleasant." Where will the soul go to look for the courage to prepare itself for such an undertaking? Only in the love of its spouse, Jesus! Let us listen to the saint:

> To conquer all the desires and renounce pleasure in everything ... with the love of which the will is wont to be inflamed ... it must have another, more living flame, a higher love, which is precisely the love of its spouse, so that the latter, replacing in it the soul's own pleasure and strength, the soul may be reclothed with courage and constancy to crush easily every other love.
>
> In order to conquer the strength of the sensitive appetites, then, just any love for its spouse is not enough, but it should also be inflamed with keen desires and loving impulses.

For St. John of the Cross, nothing is done without the love of Jesus, and for that reason, the soul's first preoccupation should be to procure this love for itself with prayer, meditation, pious reading, and sacrifice, since to favor and aid it, the grace of God will not be lacking. Yet obviously, when the soul loves Jesus, it gladly takes Him as master, and here the saint expounds how Jesus teaches with doctrine and with example to enter on the way of renunciation.

The doctrine of our saint is evangelical. If it were not, it would truly not merit our confidence, because, in the spiritual life, there is only one master: Christ Jesus. All others apply His doctrine only to particular conditions of time, state, vocation, and so forth, but the substance given is always from the doctrine of Jesus. The doctrine of St. John of the Cross on total spoliation would not, therefore, merit our adhesion were it not contained in the holy Gospel. But there is nothing to fear, since we find it there in a more formal manner.

"If any man would come after me," Jesus teaches, "let him deny himself and take up his cross and follow me" (Matt. 16:24).

Follow where? Even to annihilation, even to nothingness.

"For whoever would save his life will lose it, and whoever loses his life for my sake will find it" (Matt. 16:25).

Jesus says: "How narrow is the way that leads to life."

Yes, "the gate is narrow ... that leads to life," and alas "those who find it are few" (Matt. 7:14). For that reason, Jesus wished to add example to words, and good teachers do as He did.

We see, therefore, that St. John of the Cross saw in Jesus the model of the soul, as much in the purification of the senses as in that of the spirit—that is, in both periods of the spiritual way. As for mortification of the senses, it is certain that He died with regard to the life of the senses—spiritually during His whole life and materially at the hour of His death. In life, as He said, "He had nowhere to lay His head, and much less in death" (*Ascent* II, VII, 8). Remembering most tenderly the painful torture of the head of Jesus on the Cross, who, recalling the sufferings embraced for us by the beloved master, will not then have the strength to impose on himself some sacrifice for love of Him?

The saint continues, alluding to the second part of the journey, certainly more painful than the first. Here he draws a touching picture of the total annihilation of Christ at the hour of His death:

In reference to the spirit, it is certain that, in His last moments He was annihilated in soul, being left by the Father without any consolation or comfort ... so much so that on the Cross He exclaimed in that sorrowful lament: "My God, my God, why have You forsaken me?" (Matt. 27:46). The loving Lord was vilified and humiliated in everything:

as regards the reputation of men, since, seeing Him die on the trunk of a tree, ... they mocked Him; as regards nature, since, in it, He was annihilated, dying; and concerning the spiritual comfort of the Father, who, in those moments, abandoned Him so that He might pay the debt of human sins and unite man to God. (*Ascent* II, VII, 8)

Let us not forget that Jesus endured all that and suffered for us! "For love of us and for our salvation He came down from heaven ... and was crucified, suffered, died, and was buried" (from the Creed).

Yes, Jesus gave us the example of total annihilation, but He also made us understand that this annihilation should bear fruit.

Indeed, He then wrought a greater work than He would have done in life with miracles and striking prodigies: the work with which He reconciled and united mankind with God by means of grace. (*Ascent* II, VII, 8)

And this aspect of Jesus' annihilation also teaches us:

From this the spiritual man understands the mystery of the life of Christ in order to be united with God and knows that the more one is annihilated for His love, according to the two parts, sensitive and spiritual, so much the more is one united to Him and so much the greater is the work accomplished. (*Ascent* II, VII, 8)

Placed in the crucible of the night of the spirit, the soul will find comfort not only in the example of the sufferings of Jesus, embraced for our love, but also in the remembrance of their fruitfulness; and such fecundity will never be lacking—the saint definitely affirms this—to the sufferings of the soul.

Concentrating our attention on the teaching and example of Jesus, St. John of the Cross has prepared us to face with greater courage the inevitable trials of the spiritual way. The help that we are to receive from Jesus is not limited to this; He also has to communicate to us the grace that makes us live the supernatural life and, conforming us to Him, finally makes us reach union with God. The saint inculcates this truth, presenting Jesus to us as the spouse of the soul.

Jesus, Spouse of the Soul

St. John of the Cross, following in this the example of many mystics, always loved to present the union of the soul with God under the symbol of the nuptial union. For that reason, he speaks of espousals and spiritual marriage, and so likewise, he speaks of the spouse of the soul. Note it well, for St. John of the Cross, this spouse is always the Incarnate Word, Jesus Christ, at the same time God and man. And the soul is desirous of union with the entire Christ: with the sacred humanity, receiving from Him such abundance of grace that its life becomes like a prolongation of that of Jesus; and then also with His divinity, since it has to lose itself in the divine will, so as to be able to say with St. Paul: "I live, now not I, but Christ lives in me" (see Gal. 2:20).

For St. John of the Cross, the concept of spouse attributed to the Incarnate Word is not just a poetic figure. The saint is a theologian and knows the value and tenor of the concept in the theological tradition, especially in that which has its origin from St. Thomas Aquinas. For St. Thomas, the doctrine of the union of the soul with Christ as a bride with the bridegroom expresses the same reality as that which is contained in another figure of scriptural origin that has become most familiar to the theologians and also to spiritual persons of our time: that of the Mystical Body of Christ and of the union of this body with its head. Except that, while the Mystical Body indicates all souls together united to Christ, when one speaks of the spouse, it is usually, although not always, a matter of just one soul. In each case, an allusion is made to the communication of life from Christ that is superabundant in souls. It can be said that Christ, incorporating humanity, making it His Mystical Body (by right and by fact), contracts a mystical espousal with humanity, but since humanity includes single souls, it is also said legitimately that Christ is the spouse of every soul that becomes incorporated in Him.

St. Thomas noted that the spouse exercises his influence on his bride by right of head. We who are acquainted with the magnificent encyclical published in 1943 by the Holy Father Pius XII on the subject of the Mystical Body[9]—a veritable monument of spiritual doctrine, of which no soul of interior life should be ignorant—know the wealth of intimate relations between Christ and the soul that is expressed in this concept.

St. John of the Cross was not unacquainted with the doctrine of the Mystical Body. That is evident not only from some explicit and most beautiful allusions that we find in his major works, but also from some "romances" that he wrote during his harsh imprisonment in Toledo. In these, he clearly expresses the idea that souls attain participation in divine life and also in divine beatitude by means of their incorporation in Christ.

On this subject, we should not expect from the Mystical Doctor all the precise doctrinal statements defined by modern theologians who have made this subject the principal object of their study. But St. John of the Cross, as a talented theologian, certainly had at least the intuition of the total dependence of our spiritual life on Christ, who, in the most rigorous sense, is its true source.

All the communication of the life of grace to our souls comes to us from Christ. This is so not only in the sense that Jesus, by means of His most holy Passion, recovered for us divine grace, which the

---

[9] *Mystici Corporis Christi* (June 29, 1943).

sin of Adam — and after that, all our personal sins — had made us lose, but also because, having acquired it on the Cross twenty centuries ago, Jesus is distributing it to us at the present time.

In the redemptive work with which Christ procured our salvation and our holiness, there are, in fact, two phases. First is the suffering that Christ knew here on earth, which ended with His cruel immolation on the Cross, by means of which He acquired graces for sinful mankind. This first period is followed by another, which will last forever, in which Christ — risen, ascended to heaven, and seated at the right hand of the Father — intercedes continuously for men, so that from the immense treasure of grace acquired by Him, the particular graces of which each of us has need are taken and distributed. The above-mentioned encyclical presents to us Christ, who, in heaven, selects these graces for us, obtains them from His Father, and communicates them to our souls.

It is in this way that, in our supernatural life, we are continually under the influence of Christ, from whom our souls derive the grace that assimilates us progressively to Him. In the waters of Baptism, in which he is regenerated, the Christian is incorporated in Christ, drawing from the sacred font the principal of the supernatural life that Jesus merited on the Cross and that He communicates to the Christian by virtue of the sacrament.

This life assimilates us so much to Him that the Christians of the first century, as attested by the moving records of the catacombs and the writings of the apostolic Fathers, loved to use one symbol to express both the faithful and our loving Redeemer. This was the figure of the fish: a symbol of the Christian because, in the baptismal bathing pool, the soul drew life, and therefore, like the fish, found in the water its beginning of life; and a symbol of our Lord in the Greek initials of the words: "Jesus, Christ, Son of God, Savior," which form the word "fish."

Union with God

The likeness of the Christian to Christ is a vital likeness that is ever more accentuated with the development of the life of grace in the soul. This life unfolds under His influence and stamps in us His adorable resemblance. In the thought and desire of God, we correspond to a divine model. The heavenly Father has created us in the image of His Son, fixing His regard on this divine model who presents infinite imitability, and has called us to bring into being a particular likeness to Jesus Christ, a likeness with which we shall glorify God during our earthly life and in heaven. In fact, we read in St. Paul: "Those whom he foreknew he also predestined to be conformed to the image of his Son, in order that he might be the first-born among many brethren" (Rom. 8:29).

God has not assigned to anyone, in life, the same career; each one, says St. John of the Cross, "is guided by God along a different way, and there is hardly found one spirit that in its manner of proceeding is halfway like that of another" (*Living Flame* III, 59). We heard from the august voice of the vicar of Christ Pius XI, on the occasion of the celebration of the Holy Year of Redemption, that "star differs from star, that is, as the stars of the physical heavens, so it is in the heaven of spiritual perfection, in the heaven of the saints, each soul is singularly known, singularly loved, singularly gifted, singularly guided by God." And if, as the naturalists say, no flower is ever perfectly similar to another flower, in the supernatural order these differences are much more accentuated. Each one has to be a particular copy of Christ: in this likeness to Christ, in the divine plan that man is called to carry out, is revealed the nobility and grandeur of the human person, because each soul can repeat: "No one can be for the Lord what I ought to be for Him."

The grace derived from Christ tends, therefore, to assimilate our souls to Jesus. Grace conserves in us the identical nature that it has in the soul of Christ. By means of grace, He, being the man-God—namely, man gifted with divine personality through the hypostatic union—can also merit it for us. For that reason, this grace of the soul of Christ is called "capital grace"—that is to say, grace of the head that diverts it to the members; but in the members, it does not have a different character from that which it has in the head, although it is found in much different measure in each soul. In the soul of the Christian, grace has the same vitality and the same tendencies that it has in the soul of Christ; it tends to unite our souls to God, making us live and work to the glory of the Most Holy Trinity and for the salvation of souls.

From this, it follows that, in the Church—that is, in the society of Christian souls—the life of Christ is reflected and is prolonged to such a point that the Holy Father Pius XII thought it opportune to repeat with the ancient tradition that "the Church subsists almost like a second person of Christ," as another Christ, who is the perfect image of Him and continues His work. Like Christ, the Church not only preaches, governs, and distributes the sacraments, but shines with all the virtues of Christ, all His holy and heroic works, His zeal for the glory of the Father and for the salvation of souls.

It is to be noted however, that the Church is the sum total of separate, individual, and personal souls; the Church, therefore, would not reflect the virtues and supernatural gifts of Christ if these were not found in the individual souls. If, therefore, the Church is the perfect image of Christ, who prolongs His life in her, it also means that the life of Christ is reflected and prolonged individually in many souls. In a most beautiful prayer of one chosen soul, Blessed Elizabeth of the Trinity, a prayer that in our days has been greatly relished by spiritual persons, we find expressed this concept that corresponds to the aspirations of many souls: "To become for Christ a prolongation of His humanity, in which He can renew His Mystery of glorification of the Father and of the salvation of souls."

No ideal can be more beautiful than this for a soul espoused to Christ! In such participation in the life of its spouse, we see the fullest completion of its assimilation to Him, which is the fruit of Christ's operation in it, by means of the communication of divine grace.

That St. John of the Cross perceived by intuition these splendors of the life of divine grace in the soul and its derivation from Christ, we see from the fact that in *The Spiritual Canticle*, he explicitly attributes to Christ the communication of virtues made to the soul and of the highest life of union with God, in which the virtues stabilize it, when their development is perfected. St. John of the Cross even declares that the aureoles that in heaven adorn the eminent saints, the martyrs, the virgins, and the doctors, unite to form around the head of Christ a splendid diadem, as if to attest that all the grandeurs of the saints derive from Him and for that reason they also sing the glory of Christ.

It cannot be denied that St. John of the Cross must have had a profound sense of the influence exerted by Christ on the soul, whom He leads to union with the divinity, rendering the soul's life progressively more like the life He lived in His most holy humanity, until finally the soul becomes the perfect image of this humanity, which it not only reflects but reproduces and prolongs.

The loving gaze of the soul remains, then, on Christ, not only to see in Him the model that it is to copy, but also to beg Him to exercise His sanctifying influence completely on it, to protest to Him that it wants to let itself be docilely guided by Him and that it will obey in all things the will of its spouse.

Consequently, a whole life of intimacy with Christ is opened up to the soul, and for that reason, it is opportune to consider for a moment whether such a life of intimacy with Christ is possible for a soul that is becoming contemplative.

Jesus, Object of Contemplation

It has been said many times, and some have wanted to attribute such an opinion also to the Mystical Doctor, St. John of the Cross, that when a soul becomes contemplative and unites its spirit to God, it needs no longer occupy itself with the humanity of Christ. We know that St. Teresa of Jesus showed herself very much averse to such doctrine, and this would already suffice to incline us to think that the theologian of Teresian spirituality could not disagree with her on so important a point. So, it is to be believed that St. John of the Cross, like the holy Reformatrix, wanted the contemplative soul in its whole spiritual journey to continue to nourish an ardent devotion to Christ, never wishing to be separated from Him. Nevertheless, it is not without interest to investigate from the documentation left by the saint whether we can prove that he actually directed souls in that way.

It cannot be denied that the soul that becomes contemplative feels itself attracted in a particular way toward the divinity, and this should not cause wonder, since the first object of mystical knowledge is precisely the divinity: God. We know that contemplation is a way of knowing divine things by means of love, by means of an intense love of charity in which the soul, so to speak, experiences the One who draws it to Himself. But the object of this love of charity that draws and conquers the soul is really the *divine amiability*, God Himself, who is revealed in an obscure manner in contemplative knowledge, in which is given to the soul, as we have already said, the "sense of God." For that reason, the soul that is enjoying contemplation spontaneously keeps itself in a general loving attention and does not feel any desire to descend to particular considerations, not even to meditate on the mysteries of Christ that previously nourished its interior life so much. Can it be blamed for that?

Union with God

In no way! St. Teresa, who insisted so much on our necessary union with Christ, never asserted that a soul that, when in prayer, feels itself drawn by God to remain with Him, occupied solely in gazing at Him with love, ought to force itself to return to the consideration of Christ's humanity. What she did not concede was that the soul should seek to procure such contemplation for itself, wanting to dismiss from itself every concrete thought, and not wishing thereby to turn its gaze to Christ, for fear that this exercise would constitute an obstacle to contemplation. What St. Teresa rejects is the soul's deliberate distancing of itself from Christ with real and studied application, and not, of course, the spontaneous concentration on God, from which it follows that the soul then does not think of Christ.

This last attitude cannot really present any drawbacks, because, in order to give Christ the place that belongs to Him in our spiritual lives, it is not necessary that we think of Him all the time. It suffices that the thought of Him comes back to us frequently, in such a way as to make us habitually conscious that our spiritual life develops under His influence.

From the teachings of St. John of the Cross, as we shall now see, it becomes evident that he wishes absolutely that in the spiritual life we continue to nourish ourselves with the remembrance of Christ. For the saint, to go to Christ does not at all constitute an obstacle to contemplation; and contemplation itself, on the other hand, often serves to enlighten the soul to a great degree with regard to the mysteries of the Incarnation and Redemption.

After all we have seen in the teaching of St. John of the Cross concerning Christ as our beloved master and model, and how He remains master and model throughout the entire journey to union — which, in its various stages, accompanies the soul's gradual introduction to contemplation — it is evident that the saint does not wish to distance us from Christ at any point along the way. If we are not willing to support ourselves with His sweet remembrance, we shall not be able to find in His example the light and comfort that the saint expects from Him for the soul.

Consequently, we cannot think that the saint could have approved a studied putting aside of the thought of Christ. Of that there is no doubt whatsoever.

But what shall the soul do at the time of prayer? Should it not at that time put from its mind the remembrance of the humanity of Christ in order to immerse itself more easily in the divinity?

To respond adequately to such a question, we shall begin with saying that it clearly follows from the life of the saint, and also from one of his most typical poems, that he did not believe at all that addressing oneself to the person of Christ to begin prayer could hinder the development of contemplation in the soul. He greatly loved to recollect himself in prayer in the Eucharistic presence. In the reformed Carmel, not only through the influence of St. Teresa but also through that of St. John of the Cross, the custom was introduced of always making mental prayer in the presence of Jesus in the Blessed Sacrament, a presence that gives Him wholly to us, man and God.

Even more, the beautiful poem that the saint entitled "Song of the Soul That Is Delighted to Know God by Faith," to which we referred above, shows us that the soul is indeed nourished by the Eucharistic presence with the obscure contemplation of the divinity:

> This eternal fount lies hidden
> In this living bread to give us being,
> Although it is night.

> Here it calls to every creature
> By this water to be sated, though in darkness,
> For it is night.

Union with God

This living fount that I desire
In this living bread of life I see,
Even in the night.

It is clear that even when contemplating the Sacred Host, the soul of John was engulfed in the divinity.

To explain better how it is possible to be exalted by obscure contemplation regarding Jesus Christ, let us take note that, speaking of the consideration of Him, we more often speak of His humanity in too abstract a manner, as if it were separated from His divine personality. In reality, the soul never considers it as separated; when we speak of the humanity of Christ, we mean "Christ-man," which is not such if, in concrete, it does not presume the union of the divine person with the human nature. In short, the Christ-man is the Incarnate Word. In this concrete person who is called Jesus there is the entire humanity, but precisely because His person is divine, His divinity is also there. The principal beauty in Jesus is His divinity, and this is always grandeur and beauty in Christ.

The soul enamored of Jesus seeks to know Him as profoundly as possible and dwells spontaneously on His greatest beauties. Therefore, the gaze of the soul loving Christ and coming close to Him in the Eucharist, where He is "everything," naturally turns to His divinity. The soul, approaching Christ, also finds in Him, in a direct manner, the principal object of contemplation: the divinity that nothing now hinders the soul from enjoying with loving attention; and yet what brought it to this loving suspension was the gaze upon the tabernacle, the gaze upon the Sacred Host. The thought of Christ is not an obstacle to contemplation, although the soul makes use of it as a starting point to orient itself toward divinity.

But that is not all: not only will the remembrance of the Incarnate Word be able to move us to contemplation, but in its turn the contemplative knowledge can enrich our understanding of the mystery of the Incarnation, giving us a greater esteem of its loftiness, and ending thus in a still more profound "sense" of the divine mercy. If the contemplation of the divinity gives us here a sense of God richer than any conceptual knowledge procured for us by our intellect, we will not lose this sense of God when our regard descends from the divinity to the mystery of the Incarnation. Understanding better the unique grandeur and divine sovereignty that we have enjoyed, the humility of the God made man will appear still more touching to us, and the unfathomable divine mercy that would move our God to abase Himself so completely will be made magnificently clear to us.

St. John of the Cross, in *The Spiritual Canticle*, has spoken explicitly of this mutual, illuminating influence that, in the contemplative light, the knowledge of the divinity and of the mystery of the Incarnation exert, when the soul is joined in union with God and enjoys unitive contemplation. The saint writes that the soul and its spouse, Christ,

> both shall enjoy the savor and the delight occasioned by the knowledge, not only of the mysteries of the Man-God, but also of the virtues and divine attributes, as justice, mercy, wisdom, power, charity, etc., that are discovered in God by means of the said mysteries. (*Canticle* XXXVII, 2)

A more profound knowledge of the divine attributes is thus produced by the more profound penetration into the mysteries of Christ, and in time makes for a better understanding of the grandeur of the Incarnation.

It is understood that even though it be in the lesser degree, the same can be verified in moments of less lofty contemplation, simply because from contemplation there always proceeds a sense of God that makes the soul understand more profoundly His greatness, wherever it is found. In the mystery of the Incarnation, it is found united to the humanity in the Person of the Word.

St. John of the Cross has made us see in Jesus the master who is to guide us and also the spouse who makes our soul His spouse, whereby He shares His life, nourishing it (our soul) with His divine grace, which assimilates it to Himself and renders it in such a way fit to be united to God. The soul, with confidence and love, turns continually to its divine spouse, making known to Him its own desires, needs and hopes.

In every strophe of *The Spiritual Canticle*, which describes the entire journey of the soul toward union and finally the very life of union, we find the soul in loving communication and conversation with its spouse, Jesus Christ. Consequently, it is not a matter of never abandoning Him, but rather of knowing Him better, and above all, of understanding the highest beauty, which is His divinity. Relished in contemplation, this beauty inspires the soul with still greater love of its spouse, who, to procure life for it, deigned to hide His greatness under the veil of humanity. Jesus will always be its guide, admired and loved, its light, and its strength. Even though so weak, the soul will become strong because it is supported by His strength.

Thus, *with loving abandonment, supported by its Beloved* (see Song of Songs 8:5), it will, without fear, face the hostility and obstacles of the way: it is no longer alone! Like St. Thérèse of the Child Jesus, also in the subterranean darkness, neither seeing nor understanding where He is leading her — yet Jesus knows — full of confidence in Him, the soul feels secure that He will guide it well and lead it to the blessed end.

9

The Dark Night

Why the Purification Is Called "Night"

The long work of purification by means of which the soul prepares itself, and is also passively prepared, for union with God, is a work whose darkest, most painful period we are about to study. It came to be called by our saint, in its totality, by the name "night." He is ever speaking of the "dark night" that leads to "union." Even at the beginning of the work entitled *The Ascent of Mount Carmel*, which describes methodically, in its various active and passive phases, this prolonged work of spoliation — the work of which the book entitled *The Dark Night* is an integral part — he wanted to justify this name. It can be said that to practice renunciation and mortification is to put our powers in darkness with regard to that in which they naturally take pleasure. If we consider the spontaneous movement of our faculties, we see that they tend to occupy themselves with objects that give them satisfaction: the eye takes pleasure in beautiful things, the ear enjoys the harmony of sounds, the sense of smell delights in the sweetness of perfumes. We gladly go in search of such satisfactions because we tend to enjoy them.

When our tendency to happiness — in itself the opposite of hurtful, because it thrusts the soul toward God, our highest good and absolute happiness — seeks its food in these delights (of sense), it provokes in the soul the issuing and establishing of many attachments to created goods, which bind the spirit that expands and rejoices in them and arrests its generous upward impetus.

Now that we have studied the teachings of the holy doctor, we know how necessary it is to free ourselves from these attachments and consequently to mortify our tendencies, depriving our faculties of those objects in which they take pleasure, or at least rectifying the use that they make of them, by learning not to fix the attention on the delight that they procure and by clarifying our intention of using them according to the good pleasure of God. Naturally, in this moderate and sober use, the dazzle of the senses disappears, and the exhilarating vibrations of the spirit are mitigated. It may happen that "this fascination for frivolity," as the Holy Father Pius XI commented in one of the memorable discourses of the Holy Year of Redemption, will also draw souls that are "without deceit, without malice," with the result that "it obscures the good." That is, makes one lose the sense of the true good, the true light of the intellect, through which, after such suggestions, one can no longer know where the good is.

To deprive the senses and the spirit of this vivacity, of this vital joy that comes from their immediate satisfaction, is truly like putting them in the dark, making them leave the banquet room. The first impression that they experience in abandoning that artificial life is like a deep night, since, in fact, the sun is not yet risen. In the generous soul that has embraced renunciation, that sense of a new life has not yet come to the surface: that sense of a new life, which the presence of the divine sun rouses, and which will inundate the soul with a joy and peace beyond comparison.

This first kind of darkness created in the soul by active mortification is increased, particularly when the Lord Himself, to aid it in freeing itself from the weight of sensibility that still occupies too high a place in its interior life, makes it fall into aridity. The soul remains in darkness concerning all the beautiful ideas and sweet emotions in which it used to delight; it truly seems that night has succeeded the splendor of the sun.

Then, when the soul begins to settle itself in contemplation—which consists in the general loving attention to God—and to create the atmosphere favorable to the growth of its new intimacy with the Lord, it applies itself to the intense exercise of the theological virtues; it certainly cannot be said that the light of creatures returns. In prayer, the development of contemplation does not bring the soul new ideas; rather, just because of this, it is called "dark contemplation." Not only during prayer, but also during the day, its application to God that results from the exercise of the theological virtues renders the soul ever more alienated from creatures. These seem always more estranged, and, in fact, they alienate themselves from the heart, since the soul does not allow any attachment at all. It follows from this that they stand aloof even from the preoccupations of the soul, which learns continually to see and love them only in God.

It might be believed that this development of the light of faith in the soul should in some way illumine it, and that therefore the darkness produced by the renunciation of the creature is then substituted by a kind of divine glimmer of light. We cannot deny that, at certain times, the soul that is making progress in contemplation can have such impressions, and that these may be experienced the more by the soul that has arrived at union with God, in which the light can abound so much as to become a sort of prelude to the heavenly "day." Before arriving at this point, however, the same communication with God, being made more intense, becomes for the soul a cause of most intense darkness, of profound obscurity, in which it suffers and agonizes. This is a darkness and obscurity in which the last dross of impurity, the last obstacles to perfect union, are removed, establishing the soul in perfect humility, and at the same time drawing down on it an abundance of divine mercies. If all the preceding periods of purification merited the name "night," particularly the period of aridity called the "night of the senses," this name obviously and for greater reason, is proper to this last part of the purification, which our saint calls the "passive night of the spirit."

The Dark Night in Secular Life

Passive night! Therefore, the darkness and obscurity are not provoked by the soul but are caused by God. The saint has insisted much on the fact that the soul, with only its personal initiative, cannot attain the purity required for union. With equal force, he has added that the Lord will not fail to come to its aid, to accomplish the work that by itself it is not capable of bringing to an end, but for which it sincerely exerts itself, as can be attested by the generosity with which it has undertaken the work of active purification.

This assurance of the saint ought to be a great comfort for persons who, living in the world, also desire to reach the holiness to which the Christian vocation invites them. Obviously, they do not have at their disposal all the ascetical aids that religious find in a life organized for the acquisition of Christian perfection. In the very practice of his vows and in the observance of rules, the religious finds a continual exercise of mortification and voluntary renunciation. Obedience, for example, practiced with perfection, makes him continually renounce his own will to do that of God, which is manifested to him by the commands of superiors and by the obligatory exercises imposed by the Rule. He finds in great part those sacrifices that will free him from attachments to creatures, daily placed at his disposal in the very arrangement of his day's work, regulated by holy obedience. It suffices that he be faithful in embracing them, since the work of spiritual purification advances by means of one's fidelity.

The person living in the world, from this point of view, finds himself in very different conditions. For the most part, he does not think of a life conformed to ascetical ends but intends rather to procure for existence the greatest possible comfort, yet according to the conditions of each family. It cannot be said that there is anything blameworthy in this. For example, one of the most holy duties of a good mother is to make family life pleasant for all those who are living at home. One must never think that this pleasantness ought to be the result only of sensible pleasures, of material comforts, of entertainment, or of luxury. On the contrary, that there should be (in this pleasantness), in great part, all that may contribute to the development of spiritual values and principally all the helps to give God His place: the first place. Nevertheless, the general tone of family life is not austerity.

From this point of view, the secular does not find in the family at home the aid that the religious receives in the convent. What is to be said, then, of the social surroundings, of the office, of the workshop or factory, where he spends so many hours of his day? Far from being surroundings favorable to the life of the spirit, they are too often places where the thought of God does not have access, if indeed they are not—and alas, they often are—places of temptations and of moral perversion.

Not being helped by his milieu, the secular who wants to live an interior life must organize his life of mortification and prayer, constructing for himself a method, a norm of life, a daily routine, imposing on himself definite renunciations, seeking to procure "spiritual direction" for himself. He can do so and, in modern times, beautiful examples show that it is not a question of a theoretical possibility. There are moving examples of such accomplishments in which we see work itself becoming the instrument of mortification and the means of raising the heart to God. And even surroundings, hostile in themselves, become a field of the apostolate in which one works by word and example, but still more by prayer and suffering. I, who have lived among young workers, united in the association of Jocists (Young Christian Workers), know by experience that these are not mere words.

The secular also, although deprived of a favorable environment, can show himself generous with the Lord and practice with energy the active renunciation that draws down the benevolence of God and hence inclines the Lord to intervene with the passive purification.

When it is a question of this passive purification, however, it must be said that the secular Christian is on the same plane as the religious. Here there is no longer any difference. In the life of the secular, there are abundant occasions of which the Lord can make use to detach his heart from creatures and make him love in God alone those things and persons that perhaps he has loved too much for themselves and to which he is attached. How many events there are and how much suffering in life, particularly in family life!

You may, perhaps, have read *The Story of a Family*, published by the Carmel of Lisieux, which narrates frankly the events of the family in which St. Thérèse of the Child Jesus was born and grew up. It was truly a family blessed by the Lord, a family of saints. One is moved by the heroism of Madame Martin, who, consumed by cancer, in the last days of the illness that undermined her life, found the almost superhuman energy to handle the needle to fulfill a business obligation. The death of four babies, the painful illnesses of dear ones, the continual concern for a child who was not easy to educate, the toilsome and indefatigable work in business, and finally a malignant cancer that destroyed her: these were the "little crosses" of Madame Martin. In these, however, the humble and fervent Christian woman was truly sanctified, in a chaste wedded life and in a family life that was certainly not deprived of comforts, but in which God truly had His place. Indeed, she sanctified herself with her crosses, because she, serene and confident, knew how to accept them from the hands of the Lord, raising her glance constantly to heaven. Oh, if all Christians would really profit by their crosses! To be sure, such persons have not been lacking in recent years. Nor are they lacking now. The Holy Father Pius XII has invited us many times to pray that good souls may know how to profit by suffering. This is one of the most beautiful of prayers!

One who can accept the cross from the hand of the Lord loves Him in earnest. The secular can do this as well as the religious. Will the Lord not do for him what He gladly works in the faithful soul, to lead it through the last trial even to the heights of union? Yes, the secular can also be led by the Lord into the passive night of the spirit.

Development of the Passive Night of the Spirit

To understand the necessity of this night for the attainment of union with God, it is well to recall what St. John of the Cross has said about pure love, to which the soul attains in the state of transformation, and to know how to distinguish the sentiment of love and its operation. In pure love, the soul is occupied only with the operation of love, with the pure benevolence toward God with which it adheres fully to His most holy will. It thus lives solely for His honor and glory. The soul is no longer preoccupied with sentiments of love — that is, with that accessory part of love, still so welcome and to which we unfortunately often attach ourselves, thus diminishing the purity of our love. We also easily seek ourselves a little in the exercise of intense love, even when it makes us feel its demands of giving and imposes hard sacrifices on us.

Union with God

When we embrace certain renunciations that cost us a great deal, we acquire a knowledge of loving truly, just because we see ourselves capable of sacrifice, as experience shows; and this is in itself the occasion of some complacence, sometimes quite secret.

To love is something that delights us, and the consciousness of truly loving generates in us joy and peace. This joy is not wrong—quite otherwise! But it is necessary that our weakness not make us attached in any way to this joy, that is in itself totally legitimate. The sentiment is not God and does not at all unite us to God, whereas we ought to love only God, and all the rest in Him. But who can free one from oneself, from these last miseries and from such hidden deceptions?

God Himself will give a helping hand to the soul that He wishes to lead effectively to perfect union with Him, requiting its generosity by accomplishing in it what of itself it is incapable: God will free it from the attachment to the sentiment of love, eradicating this from it, and thereby plunging it into a desolating darkness, in which it will anxiously wonder if it still loves its God.

St. John of the Cross has compared the passive night of the spirit to purgatory, and truly, like the purgatory after death, it is the final preparation of the soul for heavenly union with God. In this life, the purgatory of the night of the spirit disposes it immediately for the union of love. But close as is this similarity, there is a great difference: while the real purgatory consists in a material and mysterious fire that, in the other life, will consume the dross of the soul that is still in debt to the Lord, here in the mystical purgatory, love works, fire does also, but they are not created to punish; just so, this fire of love will accomplish the total healing of the soul and render it holy.

It is a matter of passive love, of that love, namely, with which the Lord draws the soul to Himself and that concentrates on Him the soul's entire will; the latter is captured and borne into God, and it does nothing but consent. When the will is captured in such a way and grasped by the Lord, there is born in the soul a certain sense of God with which, in a manner almost experiential, it understands His greatness and sovereignty. When God operates thus in the soul in a sweet way, such a sense of God is also sweet. The soul enjoys some of the "general loving attention to God," which can also end in absorbing it sweetly in Him. When the passive love is stronger and more vehement and draws the soul with violence, then it is likely that the soul's reaction may be quite different. Faced with this new experience that invades it, rather than the grandeur and the divine holiness, the soul feels all the contrast between its lowly and miserable nature and the powerful communication that it receives.

Not yet being sufficiently disposed and prepared for this more abundant divine communication, the soul experiences in this realization a particular uneasiness. Its regard, illumined by the new experience, is concentrated entirely on the inadequate dispositions of its own nature. Then it begins to see itself ugly and abominable because it is still so little conformed to this divine will that wants it entirely for itself. It feels itself impure, weak, basely human, miserable, hard, and little pliable. It seems evident to it that it has no true love of God, no love that corresponds to His invitation. It does not love the Lord. It is still full of so many wicked tendencies capable of carrying it toward creatures, of making it turn back again on itself. It feels this and is afraid of it. Oh, how abject it is before the divine gaze! An idea presents itself spontaneously and is impressed on its mind: The Lord cannot love me; the Lord is rejecting me. I will never reach union with Him; I will not be saved.

St. Teresa Margaret of the Heart of Jesus, a Discalced Carmelite of the monastery of Florence—a most pure soul whom Pius XI called "Burning Snow"—who died before having reached the age of twenty-three, left us a stupendous example of a chaste life wholly hidden in God. In the last years of her life, she experienced to the full this tremendous night of the spirit. So thick was the darkness that surrounded her soul, laying bare her personal indigence, that frightened at seeing she was not succeeding in corresponding adequately to the invitations of grace, she anxiously asked her spiritual director: "Father, will I be saved?"

She was on the eve of becoming truly holy and a saint of such purity that tradition has called her the "Lily of Florence."

The divine light of contemplative knowledge, however, cannot manifest other than reality. If the saints saw themselves so miserable and so impure, it is because, facing the absolute demands of divine love, they really were.

What, then, are we to think of ourselves, so little mortified, with so little generosity?

Immensely different is this pain of the soul in the crucible of the night of the spirit from the misery of a soul tormented by the remorse of mortal sin. This latter truly merits the indignation of God. The anger of the Lord is increased at the soul, and He threatens it with eternal repulsion, although the remorse may also be a salutary pain inasmuch as it can lead the soul to conversion and so put it back in the state of grace. In our case of the soul immersed in this spiritual night, the soul is in the grace of God, and there is much progress. Yet there are still so many miseries in the soul, although under the form of tendencies to which it has decided no longer to consent—that at the realization of the divine exigencies of total purity required for union with Him, the soul sees itself really abominable and is spontaneously convinced that the Lord cannot love it.

Oh, no! Now it no longer experiences any complacence in its love for God. This love it no longer feels. It is convinced that it does not love, and also—what torments it still more—that it is not being loved!

This impression does not correspond to reality. God loves this soul, and the most beautiful proof of His love is that He is drawing it to Himself and binding its whole will. Consequently it is not at all true that this soul does not love the Lord. Quite the contrary! Its love for God is even being developed in immense proportions.

Urged by God, who draws it to Himself with passive love, it consents fully, precisely because it wishes to love only the Lord, and so its will is ever more exclusively concentrated on the divine object. The tangible proof of it: while believing itself so miserable, so unworthy of God, so deserving to be separated from Him eternally, it would do anything to follow His love, and is quite determined to endure the most cruel death a thousand times rather than in the least to offend the Lord, so greatly does it regard Him!

This love, made of immense esteem, is the first form that passive love introduces into the soul, amid distresses of spirit. This esteem for God, far from reassuring it, rather increases the torment that derives from the fear of losing Him eternally.

This torment purifies the soul; it gives it a real hatred for all that opposes God. This hatred, taking root in the soul, expels from it all its attachments because it sees them in contrast with the divine will. Thus, progressively, it is freed from them, or rather it comes to be freed from them by the divine action. This is sometimes done more lightly, being proportioned to the current capacity of the soul, which then no longer feels that contrast and has a less vivid consciousness of its own misery. At these times, the soul is conscious of the divine action in it, and it feels a passionate love for God, a love that concentrates the soul entirely on Him and no longer permits any looking back on itself.

The time passes between these alternatives of tormenting love and impassioned love that torments the soul in another manner, demanding from the soul that it give itself, immolate itself, sacrifice itself for its God, and do the impossible by embracing the most difficult things just to please its beloved. In such a way the soul ascends the stairway of love. It will see a day in which this love, becoming perfectly pure, will introduce it into union.

A Great Grace

The passive night of the spirit, still painfully desolating the soul, is consequently a great favor of God. Rightly did the saint, in his famous poem in *The Dark Night of the Soul*, sing its praises:

> O night that guided me,
> O night more lovely than the dawn,
> O night that unites
> The lover with the beloved,
> The beloved transformed in the Lover!

This night is a dawn. It immediately prepares the day of union with God. Purifying the soul from the last dross, removing the last threads of attachments to creatures, it truly transforms the human will into the divine will, so that they are no longer two wills but only one.

With this tremendous night, the Lord has rooted the soul in humility. Making it encounter its personal misery, its complete impotence, it has instilled in the soul, by supernatural prayer, such a profound conviction of its nothingness that now it will be able to receive the higher gifts of the Lord without being tempted to complacence or pride. Without such convictions, when it sees itself granted the Lord's favors, it could sometimes believe itself to be something and nourish a subtle pride, and this would not be compatible with the state of union.

The spiritual desolation of the night of the spirit is therefore a great grace, and the soul that receives it ought, as the saint suggests, to thank the Lord for it "with its mouth in the dust." Its tremendous sufferings probably inspire us with fear, and are we perhaps afraid to incur the same? We should not forget that, in one way or another, we have necessarily to submit to this work of total purification. If it is not done here on earth, it must be in the other life, in purgatory.

Life in heaven, too, is total union with God, and no total union with Him can be realized unless the soul be purified of all its attachments and from all its imperfections. If, then, the soul leaves the world in the grace of God, but without being entirely purified of all its irregular appetites, it must necessarily be purified of them in purgatory. Is it not better to be purified in this life rather than in the next?

It is enough to reflect a moment to see clearly and come to the only logical and reasonable conclusion.

The termination of earthly life and the separation of the soul from the body also ends for us the time of meriting. For this reason, it also ends the time in which we can acquire a greater intensity of love. We know that our meritorious acts bring us an increase of sanctifying grace, and that at an equal pace with the increase of sanctifying grace, we acquire an increase of the theological virtues, especially the intensification of charity. When the capacity for meriting ceases, the capacity for acquiring a further increase of charity also terminates. Consequently the soul that is being purified in purgatory with inexpressible torments, no longer advances in love, since those pains are expiatory, not meritorious.

Quite different are the conditions of the mystical purgatory! The saint has shown us this: indeed, through an immense intensification of its love, in which passive love infused by God comes to the aid of the activity of the soul, the latter emerges purified from the last of its dross. The mystical purgatory is therefore truly accompanied by the love of God, and the soul obtains an immense increase in the intensity of its love. Could a soul that desires to love God greatly, and to love Him in eternity with a love as intense as possible, hesitate, then, in its choice? Will it not prefer to be purified in this life by means of the mystical purgatory, which so greatly augments its degree of charity, rather than be purified in the other in a purgatory of fire that would not increase its love?

It could perhaps still be objected that the soul fears not having enough strength to support such suffering sent by the Lord and that, finding itself immersed, it might lose courage, despair, and thus merit eternal damnation.

We can reply most validly that such danger does not exist. We do not mean to say that the soul in the night of the spirit is confirmed in grace; positively speaking, it could still sin, but the purifying contemplation that is acting in it draws it away from sin.

All that the soul is suffering is an effect of the communication of infused love, which, by means of the activity of the gifts of the Holy Spirit, illumines the soul with regard to its state. The soul knows that infused love and the operations of the gifts of the Holy Spirit are "operating" graces—graces that, proceeding from the divine initiative, are also efficacious; that is to say, the soul always receives from them a beneficent influence that bears it to God. In the soul thus purified is born and is developed from the first moment an intense esteem for God. It would endure death a thousand times rather than offend Him. We can see that we are thus at the antipodes of the fear of committing sin, although the sensibility can experience all the depression of discouragement and feel driven to desperation. The soul strongly enamored of God with love of esteem will not give in to such inclinations.

What can be said of one who may feel quite transported by a passion for his God? It would do the most unusual and difficult things even to give Him greater pleasure. How much more will it feel ready at least to fulfill His will! We can say that in these trials caused by the action of the Holy Spirit in the soul, the latter remains as though under the wings of God, protected by Him, and therefore it has nothing to fear. Nevertheless, there is a certain remedy for the soul for its sufferings; that is, there is a way to render them less bitter, and this is the devout recourse to Our Lady.

A great servant of Most Holy Mary, St. Louis Grignon de Montfort, has noted explicitly that Our Lady can sweeten the pains of the spirit that her faithful servants incur. That is not to be wondered at. If Our Lady can alleviate the pains of purgatory in the other world, and shorten them for those of her dearest children who showed themselves faithful by wearing the holy scapular and by regularly fulfilling some practices of piety and penance, it should not seem incredible to us that she could, with her maternal intervention, also alleviate the pains of the mystical purgatory. A filial and assiduous recourse to Mary is always of great profit for the interior life and will also be helpful to the soul in the last period of its purification that prepares it for union with God.

When the soul shall have effectively attained an interior purity, and there remains nothing more in it that is contrary to the will of God, then will be realized that divine invasion that St. John of the Cross, in his works, so insistently loves to propose by means of the symbolism of the sun that invades the house when the door is opened wide:

> If the soul then does as much as it can on its own part, namely, if it succeeds in being empty and dispossessed of all things, it is impossible that God should fail to do His part by communicating Himself to it, at least in secret silence: more impossible even than the absurd hypothesis that the ray of the sun should fail to shine in a serene sky. For, as the sun, rising early in the morning, is ready to enter your house, provided you open the door to it, so God, who did not sleep when taking care of Israel, and does not sleep at all now, will

Union with God

Himself enter the empty soul and fill it with divine blessings. God is like a sun above souls, ready to communicate
Himself to them.

Let us open the door to Him with total abnegation, and He will
invade us and transform us into Himself.

10

Transforming Union

Not many souls reach the summits of union on earth. Our saint, while lamenting it, acknowledges it. There are strong motives that urge us to describe this highest life to which a soul can attain while on earth.

The prime motive is that the knowledge of the beauties of the goal that awaits us is as a stimulus for us to tend toward it with courage and energy, despite the difficulties met along the way.

The second motive: that we can understand better that between the state of union and the contemplative life by means of which we tend to this state, there exists a sort of continuity. We should not believe that the state of union, particularly in its essence, is simply a beautiful gift that one day will fall on us from heaven. No indeed! Union is the full perfection of a life that develops gradually in us, a life that union itself comes to crown. A soul that applies itself with generosity to the practice of the contemplative life, though perhaps being still far from this blessed term of union, can nevertheless ascertain that it already possesses something of it, and that it suffices to cultivate and develop what it has already acquired, in order to be able to nourish a well-grounded hope of one day attaining it. This evidently is encouraging for the soul.

Union with God

Hence, we want to follow the Mystical Doctor even in his description of the state of union, and not just simply to know its essential element, as we have done up to now. We want to see it in all its complexity and admire the spiritual treasures often bestowed on the soul that reaches it.

Following the saint's expositions, in the state of union we will distinguish a two-fold progression, the second more perfect and richer than the first. Often the saint, using the vocabulary of the mystics who love to make use of the "nuptial" terminology to speak of union with God, calls the first spiritual "espousals," and the second, spiritual "marriage." With a terminology less symbolic we can call the first "union of the will" and the second "total union." We will see these names fully justified by the descriptions that we shall give of these two degrees of union.

Union of Will

We know that the saint possessed the art of fixing the wealth of his thought in typical and suggestive formulas, and we shall meet that art again where St. John of the Cross treats of the spiritual espousal of the soul with God—that is to say, of the union of the will.

In *The Living Flame of Love*, in which the saint makes the comparison between the two degrees of union, he characterizes the first as "the perfect *yes* that the soul says to God with the will."

It seems that the saint frequently mentions a teaching inculcated by the Holy Mother Teresa of Jesus, who, in her various works, often repeats the thought that, in a more perfect form, she expressed in *The Way of Perfection*, saying: "God does not force our will; He accepts as much as we give Him, but He does not give Himself wholly if the soul does not give itself wholly to Him."

Creating man free, God comes before a creature capable of saying yes or no; He does not wish to deprive it of this capacity inherent to its nature, and for that reason, when He makes His invitation felt, He does not force; He does no violence to the will of man, but maintains its capacity to comply with or refuse His attractions. This does not mean that He would not give weight to His requests, because some are even laws for us and they condition His friendship. Unfortunately, there are those who come to lose it just because they use or abuse their liberty, saying no to Him and committing mortal sin.

There are other divine demands that, if we refuse them, we do not lose the Lord's benevolence, yet our refusal does not make Him happy. He is displeased, and we fall into venial sin. There are also more tenuous, more delicate invitations with which He no longer manifests His orders, but His desires. One who would not accept them would not offend Him, but would that person be responding fully to the divine invitation? Certainly not; that person would commit an imperfection and would not be giving full adhesion to the divine will.

God is generous, immensely more so than we are. He began giving Himself to us when He gave us His grace on the day of Baptism, or when He restored it to us at the time of our conversion from sin. He wants us to be generous with Him: "He does not give Himself wholly to the soul if the soul does not give itself wholly to Him."

This thought in St. John of the Cross is not only a genial intuition. He gives the theological proof of it and expounds it when he explains the fundamental principle of his teaching—namely, that "to arrive at union, one must go by way of total abnegation." What does it mean to practice total abnegation if not to renounce always one's will in order to say yes to God? The saint has explained how to this total yes there is a corresponding taking possession of our will on the part of the will of God. This divine will becomes our only incentive, and from that it follows that our actions, moved by the Spirit of God and informed by divine charity, will be wholly supernatural. They will belong entirely to the order of divine grace. The saint has said this very thing in a beautiful way:

> The will of God and that of the soul being then but one, they unite in one spontaneous and free consent; the soul possesses God through grace of will, and possesses all that it can have by way of will and grace, because to its "yes," God has corresponded with the true and entire "yes" of His grace. (*Living Flame* Ill, 24)

Therefore it can very well be said that the characteristic of the first degree of union is the total yes that the soul says to God with the will.

It might come to our mind: "If this is the union of will with God, I believe I have attained it, because I truly want to do all that the Lord asks of me!"

One must go slowly. Take note that there is a great difference between wanting sincerely to succeed in no longer refusing God anything and doing this effectively. For a sincere soul to want it—that is, to desire it—it is necessary that it do so from the beginning of the spiritual way. One who would not have the ardent desire of attaining it would certainly not be a disciple of St. John of the Cross, not a generous soul. All this great desire does not suffice for one to say that he has arrived at doing always and in all things the will of God. To be able to succeed in doing this, it is necessary that there be eradicated from our souls all the attachments, all the bonds that hold us back and leave us less free to respond without delay to the divine invitation. In short: between the desire of the perfect yes and its fulfillment lies the whole work of total spoliation. Since this is accomplished gradually in the one who applies himself to it, there is also progressively effected the state of soul that, having been attained in its fullness, will realize in the soul the union of will.

This is the continuity to which we alluded at the beginning of this chapter. In the way of spoliation, the soul already participates in the life that will be fully its own in the state of union: its will is gradually assimilated to that of God.

To enable us to understand the spiritual richness of this first degree of union, let us dwell a moment on the perfection of the yes uttered by the soul. It can be said that it is perfect in breadth and in depth. It is perfect in breadth because it is extended not only to that which God commands but also to all that He desires and that gives Him the greatest pleasure. The soul always keeps its eyes open to see what is most pleasing to God and has its will ready to carry it out, cost what it may. Therefore, its yes is also perfect in depth; that is, the soul does not negligently adhere to what pleases God, nor with pettiness, as if through force, but with all the impetus of the will, happy to be able to give itself to the Lord in spite of all the repugnances that nature can feel.

In the soul that has reached this stage, love truly dominates. Love for the divine will has become its sole motive and directs everything to the honor and glory of God. The life of this soul is "unified" by the love that gives it strength to embrace heroic works of virtue; in fact, it practices generous virtue continually, succeeding in accomplishing acts truly heroic.

Since God is very generous with the generous soul, He not infrequently gratifies it with profound contemplation, which ever more ardently communicates to it the sense of the divine grandeur, of the supereminence of God, who—through His beauty, His goodness, and His mercy—is presented to it as absolutely transcending all creatures and who truly absorbs all its love.

The life of the soul that has attained union of the will with God is therefore quite perfect, and yet there is still a step to go to reach that entire perfection that is possible on earth.

Notwithstanding all its spiritual riches, the soul still exhibits some deficiencies, especially with regard to subordinating the sensibilities to the spirit. The dissent that original sin has created between these two parts of our being is so deep that, to reestablish perfect harmony, which in our first parents was the fruit of a preternatural gift, the infused virtues are not at all sufficient. We need an almost habitual influence of the gifts of the Holy Spirit, an influx that the soul does not enjoy in this first degree of the life of union. For this reason, it is still subject to certain weaknesses in its sensible part; it does not yield, but they make themselves felt and also sometimes disturb its peace. It is clear that these impressions and emotions, which are a bit too lively and are not contained within just limits by a will that should dominate them entirely, expose the soul to the risk of committing some fault through inadvertence and frailty. Not only that, but given that the devil can easily exercise his influence on our insufficiently controlled sensibility, some temptations of our ruthless enemy can also enter through the door of these too vivid impressions. So, there are still some moments in which the soul may not be conscious of the Lord and in which, indeed, He does not make Himself felt, thus leaving the soul for some length of time with a sense of isolation, and therefore with a so much greater desire of definitively finding its Lord.

This it does precisely in the second period of union, of which it remains for us to speak.

Total Union

The saint has defined the union of spiritual marriage as "a total transformation into the beloved, in which both parties give themselves in turn, the one transferring the entire possession of self to the other, with a certain consummation of union of love" (Canticle XXII, 4). This means that, henceforth, the transformation is no longer only in the will; it is "total," in the sense that it is superabundant in all the other powers, just as it is in the will, since from now on, even the sensibility is completely obedient to the spirit.

This proceeds from a mutual and perfect gift of God and of the soul. God gives Himself to the soul because He comes, so to speak, to take possession of it — that is, to establish Himself in its interior as its principal mover, taking over the direction of its life and inspiring it in all it does. Naturally, this is brought about by an abundant intervention of the gifts of the Holy Spirit, whose influence is made to be felt in all the faculties of the soul, even in its sensible part, and brings this latter back into full harmony with the spirit. God has become, as it were, the soul of the soul. He Himself becomes its principle of life, so that it spontaneously exclaims in the expression of St. Paul: "I live, now not I, but Christ — God — lives in me" (see Gal. 2:20).

This consciousness of the divine action in it generates in the soul a continual sense of the presence of God, by means of which He who possesses the soul is also possessed by it. In *The Living Flame*, the saint has admirably characterized this sense of the continual presence of God:

> Oh, how happy is this soul that always feels God reposing in its breast! He is there, in the substance of the soul, ordinarily as though asleep in this embrace with its bride, who is well aware of Him and continually experiences Him and enjoys Him. (*Living Flame* IV, 15)

So, God has truly given Himself to the soul that possesses Him continually in the measure in which such possession is realizable in this world; but now the soul, too, will give itself totally to God.

Observe that this gift will no longer be just the gift of the will to which the sensible powers are imperfectly obedient, hence remaining a gift in some way imperfect; no, this time it will be the whole being that magnificently, under the motion of the gifts of the Holy Spirit, rises to God in a wonderful concert of all the powers.

Thus the soul can sing in truth:

So is the soul engaged
with all the energy at its service ...
neither does it attend to any other office
for from now on my sole occupation is love.
(*Canticle* XXVIII)

The saint explains that now the spiritual powers are occupied only in the search for the Lord, and even the sensory part is wholly employed for the honor and glory of God:

It treats the body according to God, directing to Him the operations of the interior and exterior senses. Besides, the four passions (namely, joy, hope, fear, and sorrow) are regulated according to God; because it does not rejoice except in God, nor does it hope in nor fear anyone save God, nor is it sorrowful save in relation to God; finally all its appetites and solicitudes go out to Him alone.

Here the soul gathers by the handful the fruits of its generous renouncements, since from the beginning of its spiritual journey, it has applied itself to mortify its senses and to resist its tendencies to enjoyment, going courageously "not to the easiest, but to the most difficult, not the most tasteful, but to the most insipid, etc." Again we see realized this continuity between the state of union and the life that leads to it, which we indicated at the beginning of this chapter: in total union, the soul enjoys perfectly the dominion that, during the period of purification, it had applied itself to acquire gradually. The Lord, with the motion of the gifts of the Holy Spirit, has brought to full maturity the fruit of its efforts. Since henceforth, the will completely dominates all the powers, being wholly permeated with divine love, it is clear that, from now on, the whole life of the soul is transformed into a pure canticle of love:

Every faculty of the soul and of the body … everything, in a word, is moved by love and in love; in its activity it does each thing for love and in suffering it endures everything with the relish of love … in such a way that, in the settlement of temporal affairs, as in the practice of spiritual things the soul can always affirm that its exercise consists solely in loving. Happy life, happy state, and fortunate the soul that reaches it! (*Canticle* XXVIII, 8, 9, 10)

What we have heretofore described is the ordinary state of the soul arrived at total union with God. In it there are probably some moments in which the soul, with a more abundant communication of contemplative grace that it tastes continually in a somewhat diffused way, comes to be quite rapt in God. St. John of the Cross has distinguished in the state of total union two phases that alternate with each other. The first, which we have just described, is less exalted and remains continually, and he calls it "union according to substance" to distinguish it from the other, more exalted phase, in which the spiritual powers are borne into God with great force, and which he calls "union according to the powers."

When this latter is realized, the soul that ordinarily feels God in its depths as principle of life, which moves it habitually and holds the human will, so to speak, clasped in its embrace, perceives that its intellect, passively illumined by a divine increasingly invading movement, is obscurely penetrating the depth of God, acquiring an inexpressible sense of the divine attributes. At the same time, it seems to the soul that its will, divinely enamored, is introduced into the wake of the same divine love. Then spontaneously, with the utmost delicate "appropriation," it attributes these three manifestations of the divine life in it to the three divine Persons, from whom such manifestations truly proceed, and it thus feels itself in a certain manner sharing in the Trinitarian life. It then sees perfectly realized the promise of Jesus to the soul that truly loves Him, "despoiling itself for God of all that is not God" (*Ascent* II, V, 7) — namely, that the Most Holy Trinity will come to it and make its home within it; "this will take place by the divine illumining of its intellect in the wisdom of the Son, its will taking delight in the Holy Spirit, and the Father powerfully and strongly absorbing it in the unfathomable embrace of His sweetness" (*Living Flame* I, 15).

When the saint thinks that God invites us to such great heights, and we instead run backward to such baseness, he exclaims:

> O souls created for such grandeurs and called to them! What are you doing? What is detaining you? Your pretensions are baseness, and your possessions are miseries.... Since you are blind to so much light and deaf to such loud voices ... you remain miserable and vile, ignorant and unaware of so many blessings! (*Canticle* XXXIX, 7)

O souls created for such grandeur and called to it, what are you doing? Oh yes, we, too, ask ourselves this. We also ask — a little anxiously perhaps — if God truly invites everyone to these heights, so few are the souls that reach them.

The saint also, in his *Living Flame of Love* (written for a lady who was living in the world), asked himself the question and has not left us ignorant of the reply.

"This happens," he says, "not because God wishes that few be raised to spiritual heights — on the contrary He would like all to be perfect — but because He finds few subjects capable of enduring so sublime a work" (*Living Flame* II, 27).

The saint explains that so many souls, when God hardly begins to try them with some inconvenience or temptation, instead of recognizing and accepting it with love, quickly become impatient. They do not wish to suffer; they become disgusted with the way of virtue and return to their natural satisfactions.

"Hence," the saint continues, and these are the most terrible words he has written,

> not finding them strong and faithful in that little (the Lord) sees well that they will be much less able to endure greater things, and for that reason He ceases to purify them and to raise them from the dust by means of the labor of mortification, for which a greater constancy and strength is needed than that which they have shown. (*Living Flame* II, 27)

With the tremendous consequence that such souls no longer advance and remain buried in mediocrity.

This is why there are so few saints! We do not know how to be generous, often not even in offering to the Lord the sacrifices of our choice.

Much more frequently, we do not know how to accept those that the Lord requests and by means of which He really — let us not forget it! — comes to accomplish in us the work of purification that by ourselves we are not capable of bringing to completion. We need to have a greater spirit of faith to recognize in trials the merciful hand of the Lord, more hope in order to abandon ourselves confidently to the dispositions of His fatherly providence, more charity to adhere without limits to His most holy will. Then, aided by Him, we will attain the state of union and the purity of love that characterizes it.

Such a state is precious not only for the soul that reaches it, but the whole Church becomes a sharer of its riches — and this in virtue of the Communion of Saints, from which it follows that each good act accomplished by a member of the Church has its resonance in the whole Mystical Body of Christ. What, then, will be the influence in the Church of a soul that attains the state of union, and whose works are performed wholly under the impulse of a most intense love of pure charity? The saint does not hesitate to declare that nothing is more beneficial to the Church than this love.

"An instant of this pure love," he declares in a text now become famous, "is more precious in the sight of the Lord and of the soul itself, and of greater use to the Church than all other (external) works united together" (*Canticle* XXIX, 2).

Do not believe that this is a thought uttered in haste; on the contrary, the saint insists on it, and gives some examples:

> For this reason Mary Magdalen, although she accomplished great good with her preaching, and would have accomplished much more later on, desirous as she was to do something pleasing to her Spouse and useful to the Church, hid herself for thirty years in the desert in order to abandon herself truly to this love, thinking in this way that she would thus gain much more; so much benefit does a little of this love bring to the Church!

The saint profits by the occasion offered by the recollection of St. Mary Magdalen's way of acting, to teach those wanting to live the apostolic life that everything is not in external activity, but that this (type of life), to be fruitful, must derive from the interior life and remain under its influence. If many priests and many laypeople who assist them in their apostolic activity were to attain the pure love of the state of union with God, how much more fruitful would be their sacerdotal ministry and the works of Catholic Action![10]

If the life of a soul that has reached union acquires a great social value, this certainly does not diminish the continual increase that its personal perfection receives in the state of union. In his exposition of the verses of *The Living Flame of Love*, the saint has

---

[10] The Catholic Action movement, begun in the latter part of the nineteenth century, sought to promote a Catholic influence in society. —Ed.

magnificently explained how in such a state the soul longs for eternal life, of which it is almost given a foretaste, especially in moments when its contemplation, becoming more intense, enraptures it in God. The flame of divine love that bears it to the Lord is so impetuous that it seems it ought to break "the last veil" of separation between the soul and eternal beatitude. This "last veil" is the very connection of the soul with the body and itself, and when one has reached such a degree of holiness, it is truly the only impediment that separates it from the fruition of heaven.

The one who reaches such a state, as the saint declares explicitly, does not pass through purgatory, and death immediately opens to it the gates of heaven. The Mystical Doctor explains that death itself is caused more by the impetus of love than by natural causes. Even though it may die during an illness or in the fullness of years, the soul is not torn away by these, but by "some impetus or loving encounter more sublime and powerful than the preceding, which succeeds in tearing away the veil and bearing off that jewel of a soul" (*Living Flame* I, 30).

When writing these lines, the saint was doubtless remembering the death of his spiritual mother, St. Teresa, a death unforgettable by all those who were present. When I had the good fortune to study this event in the historical documents and in the processes of beatification, I was profoundly impressed. The saint died in a rapture that lasted fourteen hours, during which her face "of fire and flame" reflected what was taking place in her soul: she appeared to be in conversation with the Lord, sweetly moaning with love, and thus she departed from this life.

"She was shining like the sun," recounted Sister Maria of St. Francis, who assisted at the scene.

Not less luminous was the death of our saint. He knew the day and hour of his passing. During the last week, he often asked what day it was. When Friday came, he let them know that that very night he would go to chant matins in heaven. He was more recollected than ever and kept his eyes closed; when opening them, he gazed sweetly at a crucifix that was near him. At 5 p.m. he received the Anointing of the Sick (the holy oil), and then, taking the crucifix in his hand, he was again absorbed in God. When he opened his eyes, he kissed the feet of Jesus. They were then ringing the nine o'clock bell.

"There are still three hours," he said and sent the religious to rest, advising them that he would have them called.

At ten, hearing the bell of a nearby monastery that was ringing for matins, he mentioned: "Through the mercy of God I am going to recite it with Our Lady in heaven," and he thanked the Blessed Virgin for his being able to die on Saturday.

Being in fervor of spirit, he recited from time to time some verses of the psalms and then asked that they read to him some passages from the Canticle of Canticles. "What precious stones!" he exclaimed when he heard the verses repeated.

He was speaking softly with his crucifix when a brightness surrounded his body, and in the midst of this light he was seen as though in rapture for love of God. The bell of the convent began to ring. The saint asked:

"What is that bell?" and they replied:

"For matins."

"I am going to say it in heaven," he answered, and again kissing the feet of Jesus, he expired.

Saturday had just begun, the fourteenth of December 1591.

"Only the honor and glory of God," the saint had written on the summit of his "Mount" of perfection.

In his last moments, he, too, had no other thought: to go and sing the praises of God in the eternal "matins." The impetus of pure love that took him from life on earth introduced him into the kingdom of infinite love.

Precious in the sight of the Lord is the death of His saints [he had written in the *Living Flame*] because in it are gathered together all the riches of the soul, and into the ocean flow the rivers of its love, which are so swollen and vast that they really seem like seas. Then are united the first and last treasures of the soul so as to accompany it at the moment it is going to depart for its kingdom, while from the farthest confines of the earth resound praises which are the glory of the just. (*Living Flame* I, 30)

May the Lord grant that we die, if not of love, at least in the love of God; our salvation would thus be assured. But why content ourselves with this, if the Lord invites us to aspire to greater blessings? Why should we put any limits, when He does not? Why not give God the place in our lives He merits and requests for His glory and for our good, the first place, which subordinates to Him all the rest? It would be quite just; it would introduce us into His peace. Alas, how often we forget our heavenly Father, who wishes us so much good! And how true is that which the saint wrote: "Jesus Christ is very little known by those who call themselves His friends" (*Ascent* II, VII, 12)!

When he is speaking of renunciation, of that liberating renunciation that gives place to God and leads to union with Him, these friends no longer want to know about His doctrine! So they don't get halfway! Few are the souls that reach union, but not because God does not want it (rather, "He would like all to be perfect," wrote the saint), but because we do not want it. The vocation to holiness is universal, but so too is the law of renunciation. Only the "nothing" leads to the "all." Here there is no distinction between secular or religious; both are invited to the same fullness of spiritual life.

The soul should empty itself as regards the will, perfectly and voluntarily, of all that to which it can be attached ... and this is its part. As for God, who will hinder Him from doing what He desires in the soul that is resigned, annihilated, and despoiled? (*Ascent* II, IV, 2)

God is like a sun over souls, ready to communicate Himself to them. (*Living Flame* III, 47)

It suffices that they open the door of their house, of their interior temple, with total renunciation, and the divine sun will enter and transform them.

To work, then, with generous efforts!

Let us free our hearts from earthly attachments. The Lord will do the rest and bring us to happiness in the serene peace of His kingdom of love.

Father Gabriel of St. Mary Magdalen

Adrian De Vos, born in Belgium on January 24, 1893, after success-
fully completing his studies in the classical humanities at Oude-
naarde, entered the novitiate of the Discalced Carmelites at Brugge
on September 2, 1910, receiving the name Brother Gabriel of St.
Mary Magdalen de' Pazzi. The following year (September 8, 1911),
he pronounced his simple vows. Shortly after that, he began his
studies of philosophy at Kortrijk, where, on September 8, 1914,
he made his solemn profession. That same day, by order of his
superiors, he left for Dublin, Ireland, together with some confreres.

Called to arms (September 1915), he had to interrupt his theological studies begun in Ireland to serve in the Belgian army during
the First World War. He was wounded twice while fulfilling his
duty of assistance in the medical corps, meriting the Cross of War
and the Medal of Victory with a citation in the army's record of
the day: "At the front for 32 months, he never ceased giving proof
of the highest spirit of charity."

When the world conflict was over, Brother Gabriel was able to
return to his beloved Carmel, and on December 20, 1919, he was
ordained a priest at Ghent.

He had hardly completed his theological studies when, in 1921,
he was appointed professor of philosophy at Kortrijk. While he was

carrying out his duties there, he was able to attend other courses, first at the University of Louvain and later at the Pontifical Faculty of the Angelicum in Rome.

In 1926, he was called definitively to Rome, to the reestablished International College of St. Teresa, which was his "home" until his death and was the theater of his untiring labors. From 1926 to 1931, he had the delicate office of vice rector and spiritual educator of the young levites, who were called to Rome from all the provinces of the order, there to receive a deeper, broader, more universal, intellectual, and spiritual formation.

From 1927 on, he taught dogmatic theology, and in 1931, he was appointed professor of spiritual theology. The latter became the field of his specialization, and even — after World War II — the exclusive subject matter of his teaching. From 1938 to 1940, he likewise taught sociology in two courses on Nazism and Marxism. In 1933, he began his annual conferences on the spirituality of Carmel, which brought to the attention of the public his remarkable gifts as a master of the spiritual life. In 1934 (December 14), he was appointed a member of the Roman Academy of St. Thomas Aquinas. When in 1935, by will of the Holy See, the theological faculty was erected in the International College of St. Teresa, Father Gabriel became the prefect of studies and remained in this office until 1947. In 1945 (January 18), he was numbered among the consultors of the Sacred Congregation of Rites, in which office, besides bringing to it the contribution of his profound doctrine, he was likewise able — in the study of the causes of beatification and canonization — to enrich his knowledge of the spiritual life with the experience of the saints.

In 1941, he founded *Vita Carmelitana* (a review of spiritual culture) to foster the spiritual formation of his Carmelite family. In 1947, this became *Rivista di Vita Spirituale* with a program of broader and, indeed, universal interest.

Father Gabriel of St. Mary Magdalen

In the last ten years of his life, Father Gabriel was increasingly recognized as a spiritual master, not only abroad, but above all in Italy, where, through his writings, his conferences, and his participation in numerous congresses, he became an ardent leader of the spiritual movement.

His great heart, his singular gifts as writer and teacher, he put entirely at the service of the apostolic zeal with which his soul burned.

Supported by the teachings of Pius XI, he upheld with repeated insistence that the laity are obliged to tend to Christian perfection and to the fullness of charity. It was this idea that inspired him to compose the present volume.

With the same desire of aiding the laity to find their real holiness in the exercise of their profession, he endeavored to present in clear light the probably unsuspected possibility of attainable heights, to encourage the vast number of souls that in the present-day lay world feel drawn by the greatness of the life of the spirit.

Docile to the voice of the popes, as always, Father Gabriel took an interest in Catholic Action. In 1940–1941, he gave an entire course on the spirituality of Catholic Action, with the intention of finding means to enable Catholic Action to take advantage of the great wealth of Teresian spirituality.

However, he cherished the greatest hopes for a better future in seeing the numerous groups of apostles who, among the laity, were preparing to struggle with generosity and heroism for the Church and for the spiritual values of Christian civilization. He liked to give prominence to the proper place of the laity in the apostolate, whether it was in immediate collaboration with the hierarchical apostolate, or in the exercise of professional activities, where the laity have a proper task to perform in the building up of our Christian civilization. This latter is a task in which they assume greater personal initiatives and therefore, also, greater direct responsibility.

Finally, he instilled in everyone the consciousness of apostolic duty, "the tremendous, never sufficiently meditated mystery"[11] of the responsibility of the laity with regard to the salvation of the world. "I believe that it is opportune," said Father Gabriel, "with regard to making known to the laity who live in the world, that—for all that concerns the possibility of collaboration with Christ—they belong to the same great category of Church members, to which also belong so many consecrated souls, of which there can be no doubt at all that they are bound to exercise the apostolate."

This doctrine on the apostolate, at the same time so sublime and so sensible, Father Gabriel applied in the practice of his own life, with that ardor and enthusiastic impetus that was characteristic of him. He drew his apostolic zeal from his life of deep piety and continual intimacy with the Lord. He was a man of prayer. Even when he used to return exhausted from his apostolic labors, he was most faithful to his hours of mental prayer and found there, close to our Lord, the generosity necessary to resume with vigor his day of incessant work.

He was truly a man of God, full of love for souls.[12]

—Father Benjamin of the Most Holy Trinity, OCD

[11] Pius XII, *Mystici Corporis Christi*, no. 44.
[12] From *Rivista di Vita Spirituale* (1953).

SPIRITUAL DIRECTION
⋙ SERIES ⋘

SOPHIA INSTITUTE PRESS

If this book has caused a stir in your heart to continue to pursue your relationship with God, we invite you to explore two extraordinary resources, SpiritualDirection.com and the Avila Institute for Spiritual Formation.

The readers of SpiritualDirection.com reside in almost every country of the world where hearts yearn for God. It is the world's most popular English site dedicated to authentic Catholic spirituality.

The Students of the Avila Institute for Spiritual Formation sit at the feet of the rich and deep well of the wisdom of the saints.

You can find more about the Avila Institute at
WWW.AVILA-INSTITUTE.COM.

Sophia Institute

Sophia Institute is a nonprofit institution that seeks to nurture the spiritual, moral, and cultural life of souls and to spread the Gospel of Christ in conformity with the authentic teachings of the Roman Catholic Church.

Sophia Institute Press fulfills this mission by offering translations, reprints, and new publications that afford readers a rich source of the enduring wisdom of mankind.

Sophia Institute also operates the popular online resource CatholicExchange.com. *Catholic Exchange* provides world news from a Catholic perspective as well as daily devotionals and articles that will help readers to grow in holiness and live a life consistent with the teachings of the Church.

In 2013, Sophia Institute launched Sophia Institute for Teachers to renew and rebuild Catholic culture through service to Catholic education. With the goal of nurturing the spiritual, moral, and cultural life of souls, and an abiding respect for the role and work of teachers, we strive to provide materials and programs that are at once enlightening to the mind and ennobling to the heart; faithful and complete, as well as useful and practical.

Sophia Institute gratefully recognizes the Solidarity Association for preserving and encouraging the growth of our apostolate over the course of many years. Without their generous and timely support, this book would not be in your hands.

www.SophiaInstitute.com
www.CatholicExchange.com
www.SophiaInstituteforTeachers.org

Sophia Institute Press® is a registered trademark of Sophia Institute. Sophia Institute is a tax-exempt institution as defined by the Internal Revenue Code, Section 501(c)(3). Tax I.D. 22-2548708.